access to history

Germany Divided and Reunited 1945–91

Nigel Bushnell and Angela Leonard

HODDER
EDUCATION
AN HACHETTE UK COMPANY

Study Guide author: Sally Waller (AQA)

The publishers would like to thank the following individuals, institutions and companies for permission to reproduce copyright illustrations in this book: AKG-images, page 8; © Bettmann/CORBIS, pages 15, 25, 69, 78, 83; BPK, page 156; BPK/Wolfgang Albrecht, page 53; BPK/Gerhard Kiesling, page 134; BPK/Kunstbibliothek, SMB, page 22; BPK/Klaus Lehnartz, page 67; BPK/Jochen Moll, page 84; BPK/Hilmar Pabel, page 91; BPK/Abisag Tüllmann, page 43; © dpa, page 143; © Haus der Geschichte der Bundesrepublik Deutschland, page 28; © Imagebroker/Alamy, page 142; © INTERFOTO/Alamy, page 111; Keystone/Getty Images, page 65; John Macdougall/AFP/Getty Images, page 157; Chris Niedenthal/Time Life Pictures/Getty Images, pages 120, 136; George Rodger/Time Life Pictures/Getty Images, page 2

Every effort has been made to trace all copyright holders, but if any have been inadvertently overlooked the Publishers will be pleased to make the necessary arrangements at the first opportunity.

Hachette UK's policy is to use papers that are natural, renewable and recyclable products and made from wood grown in sustainable forests. The logging and manufacturing processes are expected to conform to the environmental regulations of the country of origin.

Orders: please contact Bookpoint Ltd, 130 Milton Park, Abingdon, Oxon OX14 4SB. Telephone: (44) 01235 827720. Fax: (44) 01235 400454. Lines are open 9.00–5.00, Monday to Saturday, with a 24-hour message answering service. Visit our website at www.hoddereducation.co.uk

© Nigel Bushnell and Angela Leonard 2009
First published in 2009 by
Hodder Education,
An Hachette UK Company
Carmelite House, 50 Victoria Embankment,
London EC4Y 0DZ

Impression number   8
Year   2015

Cover photo: A gap in the Berlin Wall, Junophoto/fStop/Photolibrary Group
Typeset in 10/12pt Baskerville and produced by Gray Publishing, Tunbridge Wells
Printed and bound by CPI Group (UK) Ltd, Croydon CR0 4YY

A catalogue record for this title is available from the British Library.

ISBN: 978 0340 986 752

Germany Divided and Reunited 1945–91

Contents

Dedication

Keith Randell (1943–2002)

The *Access to History* series was conceived and developed by Keith, who created a series to 'cater for students as they are, not as we might wish them to be'. He leaves a living legacy of a series that for over 20 years has provided a trusted, stimulating and well-loved accompaniment to post-16 study. Our aim with these new editions is to continue to offer students the best possible support for their studies.

NB: *To my grandmother*

AL: *To the union of the families Leonard and Maerz 08.08.08*

Introduction: Germany 1945–91

This book is the study of how a devastated Germany in 1945 became a divided nation in 1949 and remained so for the next 40 years. During that period two German states successfully developed two contrasting models of government:

- a capitalist West Germany firmly allied to Western Europe and the USA, and
- a socialist East Germany allied to the **Eastern bloc** and the USSR.

This division seemed to have become permanent until a very rapid and unexpected chain of events from the summer of 1989 led to the formal reunification of Germany in October 1990. Today, Germany is a country still coming to terms with its turbulent past.

The key dates from the end of the Second World War to the reuniting of Germany are shown below.

Key dates

1945	April	Hitler committed suicide in Berlin
	May	The Allies accepted the unconditional surrender of Germany's armed forces
1949		The three Western zones under British, US and French occupation became West Germany (FRG). The Soviet zone of occupation became East Germany (GDR)
1955		The FRG became part of NATO followed by the GDR becoming part of the Warsaw Pact
1961	August	The construction of the Berlin Wall began
1989	November	The Berlin Wall opened
1990	October	The official reuniting of the GDR and the FRG
1991	June	The German government voted for Berlin to become the capital of a new reunited Germany

The chaos in the final stages of the war

Key question
What was the situation in Germany in 1945?

The circumstances facing Germans trying to survive in the final stages of the Second World War were horrific. Over three million German soldiers had been killed and over three million more were held as Soviet prisoners of war. In the east, the roads were full of millions of refugees trying to flee the Soviets. Soon these would be joined by a further eight million displaced foreign workers and also millions of Germans forcibly expelled from German territory in the east. Almost half the population was on the move in 1945. Germany had also suffered heavy Allied bombing raids by the USA and Britain. Whether these intensive air raids were necessary is still a controversial subject today. Many Germans feared the activities of the SS – the Nazis' élite force – whose continued fanaticism meant that any Germans seen as being defeatist were often executed. Hitler Youth members as young as 12 years old continued desperately to try and defend Berlin.

A young German boy walking past corpses from the Bergen-Belsen concentration camp in May 1945.

Key figures

Josef Goebbels 1897–1945
Appointed as the Nazi Minister for Propaganda and Enlightenment in 1933 and remained firmly committed to Nazi ideals and personally loyal to Hitler.

Heinrich Himmler 1900–45
Was in charge of the entire Nazi concentration and extermination camp system as well as head of the SS and *Gestapo*.

Key terms

Federal Republic of Germany
Otherwise referred to as West Germany or *Bundesrepublik Deutschland* with its capital in Bonn. It officially existed from May 1949 until October 1990.

German Democratic Republic
Otherwise referred to as East Germany or *Deutsche Demokratische Republik*. Its capital was referred to as East Berlin by the West, but as 'Berlin – Capital of the GDR' by the East. It officially existed from October 1949 until October 1990.

This was against a background of continuing Nazi government propaganda. Early in 1945 there were still radio broadcasts from the government announcing new secret weapons that would succeed the V1 and V2 rockets already in use. Even in early April 1945 Reich Propaganda Minister **Josef Goebbels** seized on horoscope readings to announce that there would soon be a change in Germany's military fortunes. The final stages of the war culminated in the Nazi leadership's declaration of a 'scorched-earth' policy: to destroy deliberately what remained of Germany's shattered infrastructure before the Allies entered its territory. Hitler showed no signs of remorse and blamed his armed forces and the German civilians themselves for the impending defeat of the 'thousand-year Reich'. Other leading Nazis, such as **Heinrich Himmler**, deluded themselves that Germany would be able to make peace agreements with US General Eisenhower and would then join the USA in a military alliance against the USSR. Himmler even concerned himself about whether when he met Eisenhower he should greet him with the Nazi salute or a handshake.

In this chaos, the surviving German population had to cope with a number of severe problems. They were already labelled as military aggressors. Soon they were going to be further stigmatised when the wartime atrocities committed in Germany itself and the Nazi-occupied territories, and the attempted extermination of the Jews and other groups became known around the world.

At the end of the Second World War, neither the Germans themselves nor the four Allied occupying powers (Britain, the USA, France and the USSR) had any firm idea what Germany's future would be. Thousands of Germans committed suicide at the sheer thought of being under Soviet control – a fear fanned by the relentless Nazi anti-Bolshevik propaganda under which many had grown up and had come to believe. Others, including many at the highest levels of Nazi leadership, had killed themselves fearing the repercussions for their participation in Nazi racial and social policies. In April 1945, Goebbels and his wife, spending their final days with Hitler in his bunker, had also murdered their six children before killing themselves. They preferred this to their children growing up in a Germany without National Socialism. The Allies themselves were also uncertain and divided over what Germany's fate should be. This was the situation which ultimately led to the eventual division of Germany for 40 years.

Developments in Germany after 1945

Both German states became largely successful, if not model states, in terms of their own respective economic, social and political ideologies. On the whole the **Federal Republic of Germany** (FRG – West Germany) became a stable, economically successful example of parliamentary democracy and capitalist economics while the **German Democratic Republic** (GDR – East Germany) was based on Marxist–Leninist principles and was arguably the most successful **socialist state** in Eastern Europe.

Both the FRG and the GDR became valuable members of their respective military alliances: NATO and the Warsaw Pact. Both Germanys represented the frontline of the **Cold War**. They faced each other across a heavily fortified 'inner-German' border and the city of Berlin was itself later physically divided from 1961 to 1989 by the Berlin Wall (see pages 62–71). The division of Germany most clearly exemplifies the **Iron Curtain** dividing the two Germanys for 40 years. Many Germans were brought up to see their neighbouring 'other Germany' as a hostile state, despite often having friends and family members on the other side of the border. Many East Germans welcomed visits and the sending of supplies of scarce resources, such as fruit and good coffee, from family and friends in the FRG, while at the same time having to label those personal contacts ideologically as class traitors from the neighbouring neo-fascist German state. However, as time passed and families and friends from the immediate post-war period died, the amount of contact and first-hand knowledge about the 'other Germany' obviously decreased.

Historians' views of post-war Germany

The differing historical analyses of post-war Germany are often heavily influenced by their respective Cold War considerations. Works by East German historians were in the official government sanctioned form. They denounced the FRG and they claimed the GDR was dutifully protecting its own citizens with the '**anti-fascist protective wall**'. The FRG claimed that the GDR was a brutal dictatorship and the GDR claimed that the FRG was a continuation from Nazism.

Many historians in the West portrayed the GDR simply as an oppressive and **totalitarian** regime which was under Soviet control. Even the more left-wing historians in the West did not see the GDR regime as an example of a humanitarian socialist society. Any publications in the West that portrayed a more complex picture of life in the GDR were usually written by GDR dissidents. Therefore, much history written during the period of the Cold War division of Germany has a clear political bias. Since the reunification of the two Germanys in 1990, historians have had increased access to archives and first-hand accounts. In many instances, this research has led to **revisionist** views which show a much less straightforward and more complex recent German past.

Key terms

Socialist state
In this instance, the following of Marxist–Leninist ideology by many countries in post-war Eastern Europe, which are also often referred to as communist.

Cold War
The period of hostility, but not outright war, between the USA and USSR and their Allies from the end of the Second World War until the early 1990s.

Iron Curtain
A term popularised in 1946 by Winston Churchill, Britain's wartime Prime Minister, to describe the increasing division of Europe between east and west.

Anti-fascist protective wall
The official name given by the GDR government to the inner-German border and later to the Berlin Wall.

Totalitarian
A form of government in which the state has total control over its society and people.

Revisionist
Historians whose views challenge former commonly accepted opinions.

Key question
How have attitudes within Germany changed since the reuniting of the GDR and the FRG?

Coming to terms with reunification

The painful reckoning and burden of the Nazi past has continued for several generations and is still an emotive issue in twenty-first century Germany. In 2007 for example, there was considerable controversy when it was decided to open to the public part of the Nazi war bunker system underneath Berlin. The pain and shame of the Third Reich's responsibility for the Holocaust still haunt Germany. In March 2008, discussions between Germany and Israel (between Chancellor Merkel and Prime Minister Olmert) faced fierce opposition from some Israeli MPs. The Second World War ended in 1945. But Germany was divided in 1949 and many of those Germans who found themselves growing up in what became the GDR, or had family and friends in the 'other Germany', maintain that the burdens of the Second World War were not finally lifted until the opening of the Berlin Wall in 1989.

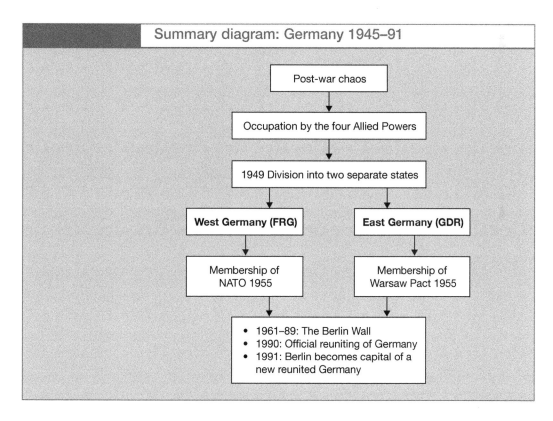

Summary diagram: Germany 1945–91

Post-war chaos

Occupation by the four Allied Powers

1949 Division into two separate states

West Germany (FRG)

East Germany (GDR)

Membership of NATO 1955

Membership of Warsaw Pact 1955

- 1961–89: The Berlin Wall
- 1990: Official reuniting of Germany
- 1991: Berlin becomes capital of a new reunited Germany

1 Defeated Germany to Divided Germany 1945–9

POINTS TO CONSIDER

In the immediate post-war years it was by no means clear, either to the Allies or to the Germans, what the future of Germany would be. The purpose of this chapter is to examine the conditions facing the Germans and the Allies in the immediate post-war period and to explore how, against a background of increasing international tension, Germany became a divided nation. Throughout this study of Germany 1945–91 it is worth bearing in mind the extent to which the Cold War determined what happened to Germany – including the reuniting of East and West Germany in 1990.

The major themes covered are:

- The seeds of Allied disagreements and tensions: the Potsdam Conference
- The conditions facing post-war Germany
- Denazification
- Developments in Germany 1945–8: the reasons for increasing division
- The establishment of two German states in 1949

Key dates

1945	May	Germany unconditionally surrendered
	July	Potsdam Conference
1946		Nuremberg Trials
1947	January	Formation of Bizonia
	March	Truman Doctrine announced
	July	US government announced the Marshall Plan
1948	June	Currency reform in the Western zones
	June	The Berlin Blockade and Berlin Airlift started
1949	May	The Berlin Blockade and Berlin Airlift ended
	May	Formation of the FRG
	August	Adenauer became first Chancellor of the FRG
	October	Formation of the GDR

Key question
What was decided at Potsdam and what issues were left unresolved?

Key dates

Germany unconditionally surrendered: May 1945

Potsdam Conference: July 1945

Nuremberg Trials: 1946

Key terms

Denazification
The process of ridding Germany of the conditions and individuals that were responsible for Nazism.

Reparations
Payments by Germany as compensation for the damage caused during the Second World War.

NATO
The North Atlantic Treaty Organisation. A military alliance set up in 1949. It was made up of countries in Western Europe as well as the USA and Canada.

Warsaw Pact
Set up in 1955 as a military alliance of Eastern European socialist states by the USSR in response to FRG's membership of NATO.

1 | The Seeds of Allied Disagreements and Tensions: The Potsdam Conference

At the end of April 1945 Hitler committed suicide and the following short-lived German government unconditionally surrendered on 8 May. On 5 June, the Allies (Britain, France, the USA and the USSR) took over joint control of all government responsibilities in the defeated Germany. A major conference was then held at Potsdam just outside Berlin in July 1945. In relation to Germany, the conference aimed to deal with four main issues: disarmament, **denazification**, territorial adjustments and **reparations**. The German issue was only part of the conference discussions and much of the time was spent discussing the war which the Allies were still fighting in the Far East against Japan. The disagreements between the Allies at Potsdam provide an insight into the different aims and priorities of the occupying powers. The Potsdam Conference contributed to the increasing tension between the Soviet leader Stalin and the Western Allies by bringing out into the open differing views and priorities.

Demilitarisation

On the issue of demilitarisation the Allies found it easy to agree. Disarmament was a relatively straightforward process because all the Allies agreed that Nazi expansionist policies had been the cause of the Second World War. This meant that the Allies agreed to the dismantling or destruction of any German factories used for building weapons or armaments, as well as the disbanding of Germany's armed forces. It was not until the mid-1950s that both German states were able to develop – and then very controversially – their own armed forces. However, by then the FRG and the GDR were firmly integrated respectively into the two rival military alliances of **NATO** and the **Warsaw Pact**.

The Nuremberg Trials

The Allies agreed to put leading Nazis on trial as war criminals. These trials took place in the German city of Nuremberg in 1946, chosen because of its close associations with the Third Reich as the scene of Nazi rallies. Hitler, Goebbels and Himmler had already committed suicide. Altogether 22 leading Nazis were put on trial. Of these, 12 were sentenced to death on 1 October 1946 (Göring mysteriously managed to obtain poison and commit suicide the night before his execution, despite being held in a prison under Allied control and intense supervision), seven were given various prison sentences and three were acquitted.

The seven Nazis who were sentenced were sent to Spandau prison, just north-west of Berlin. These included Hess, Hitler's former deputy, sentenced to life imprisonment, and Speer, Hitler's Minister of Armaments and War Production from 1942. The four occupying powers had not previously planned the prison arrangements. They eventually agreed that they would each staff Spandau prison on a monthly rotating basis and this arrangement continued for more than two decades. After Speer was released in 1966, Hess remained a solitary figure there until committing suicide in 1987. In September 2007, British government papers revealed that US President Nixon had actually been willing to release Hess in the mid-1970s, but both the British and Soviet governments opposed this as they felt that Hess showed no signs of remorse and, that, if he were released, he might become a focus for a revival of Nazi politics.

Territorial adjustments to Germany

On the issue of territory and the future of Germany, there were clear signs of disagreement. When the Allied leaders gathered at Potsdam in July 1945 the situation was very different from when they had previously met at **Yalta** in February 1945. When Roosevelt, Churchill and Stalin had met at Yalta, US forces on Germany's western borders were preparing to enter the *Reich* and military success seemed assured. There was more co-operation at this stage between the Allies as military strategy outweighed political considerations. In the following two months of fighting, the **Battle for Berlin** alone had cost the USSR more than 300,000 dead or wounded soldiers. These losses hardened Soviet attitudes with the result that by the time the Allies met again in July 1945 at Potsdam, clear differences of political opinion between them had emerged. Another significant difference at Potsdam was that, following the death of Roosevelt in April, the USA was represented by its new President, Harry S. Truman, who was a sterner anti-Communist than his predecessor. Furthermore, Churchill was replaced during the actual conference by Clement Attlee, as a result of the Labour Party's victory in the British general election in July.

Key terms

Yalta
The wartime conference of February 1945 which decided that the countries in Eastern Europe that had been invaded by Germany should be re-established after the war.

Battle for Berlin
The name commonly given to the final few months of the Second World War in Europe which led to Soviet forces finally occupying the city itself.

The Allied leaders at the Potsdam Conference, from left, British Prime Minister Clement Attlee, US President Harry S. Truman, and Soviet Union state and party leader Josef Stalin.

The discussions at the Potsdam Conference over territory most clearly showed the beginnings of tensions between the Allies. It also left certain territorial issues unresolved:

- Germany was to be divided into four zones: Britain, France (Stalin would only agree to a French zone if it was taken from existing Western zones) and the USA were to occupy areas in the west of Germany and the USSR was to occupy the east. A common joke was 'America got the scenery, France got the wine and Britain got the ruins'. The Soviet zone was the largest (40 per cent of 1937 German territory and 30 per cent of its industrial production) and significantly it included Berlin, 200 km inside the zone. The Allies decided Berlin would remain as Germany's capital, but it would also be divided between the four occupying powers. What was still unclear was if the four zones would ever form a united country again and there was no agreement on Germany's long-term future. At this point it was by no means certain, or intended, that there would be a divided Germany.

There was also much friction over Poland. At Yalta, territorial changes and compensation for the USSR had been agreed in principle. But nothing had been finalised. By the time of the Potsdam Conference, Germany east of the **Oder–Neisse** had been occupied by Soviet troops. By early 1945:

- Poland already had a pro-communist government supported by the USSR
- five million Germans had been forcibly expelled from former German territory
- parts of eastern Poland had been incorporated into the USSR.

Immediately at the end of the Second World War it was Stalin's clear intention to establish a socialist government in Poland. This would secure the USSR's western border with eastern Germany. The Allies intended that another peace conference would be held to determine the final territorial boundaries. This never took place. It was only with the reunification of the two Germanys in 1990 that Germany's eastern border with Poland was finally officially settled.

Reparations

It was also agreed at Potsdam that payment to the Allies for war damage would take the form of the requisitioning of German machinery and industrial equipment rather than financial penalties. Lessons had been learnt from the **Treaty of Versailles** about how financial reparations had contributed to problems in Germany after the First World War. Nevertheless, there was a lack of consistency in the approach to reparations amongst the Allies. Although the Western Allies were keen not to repeat the same mistakes that had been made at Versailles, the USSR had not forgotten how harshly Germany had treated Russia at the **Treaty of Brest-Litovsk** in 1918. The approach to reparations was a major obstacle to immediate economic recovery in the Western and Eastern zones and soon became a major source of tension between the Western Allies and the USSR.

Key terms

Oder–Neisse
Rivers on the eastern side of Germany.

Treaty of Versailles
The 1919 settlement that forced Germany to give up territory, pay reparations, reduce its armed forces, and accept responsibility for the First World War.

Treaty of Brest-Litovsk
The punitive peace treaty imposed by Germany on Russia in 1918.

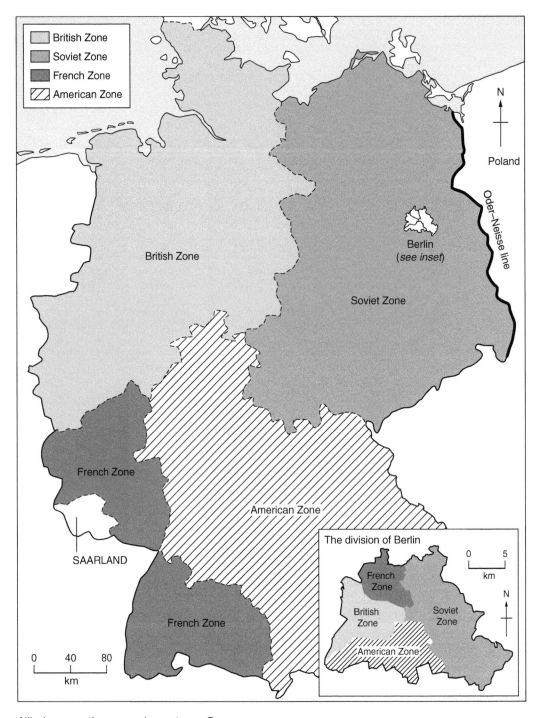

Allied occupation zones in post-war Germany.

Key question
Why were there
disagreements over
reparations?

Disagreements over reparations

Stalin's attitude

Friction quickly developed between the occupying powers over
Stalin's attitude to reparations. Stalin felt justified, following the
loss of 25 million Soviet lives and the devastation of so much
Soviet territory during the war with Germany, in transferring
entire factories, railway stock and even railway track to the USSR.
There are some estimates that up to a quarter of all industrial
goods were transferred from the Eastern zone back to the USSR.
The policy was not only applied to material goods. There were
even instances of German scientists and technological experts
being forcibly taken to the USSR, sometimes with their entire
families. From Stalin's perspective, the USSR needed to be
secured from attacks from the west. Its territory had been
occupied in three major invasions: in the Napoleonic Wars in the
early nineteenth century, and in both the First and Second World
Wars. For future Soviet security, Stalin was concerned that the
USSR should not face a resurgent Germany on one side and a
resurgent Japan on the other. It was not until 1948 that the USSR
eventually stopped dismantling factories in the Eastern zone. It
did so then only because it realised that it was highly likely that
the Soviet sector would become one of the USSR's satellite states
and thus a first line of defence against the West. The Soviet
stripping of resources from the Eastern zone was to have a long-
term effect on living standards and the subsequent development
of the East German economy.

Tension between the allies

As well as increasing anti-Russian feeling in the Soviet zone of
occupation, this stripping of Germany's resources created more
friction with the Western Allies, who were angered even more
when the USSR failed to fulfil another agreement from the
Potsdam Conference. The Western zones contained the majority
of Germany's industry while the Soviet zone was mainly
agricultural. Therefore, it was agreed that industrial goods would
be transferred to the Soviet zone, which would in turn provide
food and raw materials to the Western zones. The failure of the
USSR to keep to this agreement contributed to the severe food
shortages in the Western zones. Stalin's policy strained relations
between the Allied powers and led to retaliation. In 1946, the
USA stopped sending goods from Western zones into the Soviet
zone. The economy of the Soviet zone was also hampered by the
absence of the significant financial support that the Western zones
benefited from when the Marshall Plan (see page 23) was later
introduced. Stalin has often been presented as the worst offender
in the extraction of reparations from Germany. In fact the French,
even though they had the smallest and poorest zone of
occupation, extracted proportionately far more than the USSR.
The French maintained that because they had not actually been
present at the Potsdam meeting they could interpret its policies
more loosely.

Summary diagram: The seeds of Allied disagreements and tensions – the Potsdam Conference

Key issue	Policy at Potsdam	Result
Demilitarisation to prevent further German militarism	To disarm Germany completely	Germany was disarmed, but in 1955 both parts were in their respective alliances. This rearmament was met with opposition inside both the GDR and the FRG (see Chapter 2)
Denazification	To rid society of Nazism by preventing former active Nazis from holding influential positions in society (see page 16)	Major Nazi figures were brought to trial at Nuremberg. The USSR and the Western allies had different ideological standpoints. Overall denazification became increasingly difficult to implement (see pages 16–17)
Territorial adjustments	The division of Germany and Berlin into four zones of allied occupation. This was intended to be a temporary measure. The four zones made up an area of approximately 75 per cent of Germany's 1937 borders	The Western zones later joined together (see pages 24 and 26) and the Soviet zone was increasingly organised on Marxist–Leninist principles. No further meeting was held. Germany eventually became two separate states (see page 27)
Reparations	The West was concerned that Germany should not be treated too severely. The USSR justified compensation for the damage and costs incurred during Second World War	The issue of reparations became a major source of tension between the Western powers and the USSR

2 | The Conditions Facing Post-war Germany

The extent of post-war dislocation and suffering

More German civilians died during the period 1945–7 than during the previous six years of fighting in the Second World War. There were millions of refugees, there were serious food shortages, and the winters were severe. Food supplies had collapsed so much that there were even rumours of cannibalism. Ration levels in 1946 and 1947 were lower than they had been during the Second World War. Some German refugees arrived naked and robbed of all their possessions, having been forcibly expelled from former German territories in what had now become parts of Poland and Czechoslovakia. Many Germans experienced more precarious conditions during the period of immediate post-war occupation than those they had suffered during the Third Reich and the Second World War.

Key question
Why was there such a
severe refugee crisis
in post-war Germany?

Refugees and displaced persons

It is notable how transient much of the population in Germany was at this stage. In June 1946, for example, over half a million Germans expelled from Czechoslovakia arrived in the Soviet zone. Refugees accounted for nearly a quarter of the population in the eastern sector. Many refugees had been former prisoners in Nazi concentration, extermination, forced labour or prisoner-of-war camps. Their hardship was all the more severe because they had no possessions to trade with. During this period money had become almost worthless as a form of currency and had been almost entirely replaced by goods such as potatoes or cigarettes. Displaced Persons Camps existed for many years in post-war Germany. Some of them were on the sites of former Nazi concentration camps, such as Dachau, near Munich. The last Displaced Persons Camp did not close until 1957.

To begin with the Allies tried to repatriate as many displaced persons as possible to their home country. Many did not want to return to those countries in Eastern Europe that were now setting up socialist governments and were becoming part of the USSR's system of satellite states. The USSR, however, demanded that any refugees in the Western sectors who had at some point been Soviet citizens must return. The Western Allies complied with this request. The principle of displaced persons' returning to their home country was a clearly a dilemma for the German Jewish survivors of the former Nazi camps because many were already in their home country. Many felt very uncomfortable about rebuilding their lives in a country which had tried to exterminate their entire race, and many also felt uneasy about emigrating to Palestine and the politics of **Zionism**.

Over time those displaced persons who could not be repatriated found new homes – especially in Britain, Canada, France, Germany, Israel and the USA. By the early 1950s, the FRG had set up a system for West German universities to accept a quota of displaced persons as students.

Key term

Zionism
The movement for
establishing an
independent state
of Israel.

Initial post-war Allied occupation of Germany

Key question
Why was there
resentment of Allied
occupation?

The initial occupation of Germany by Britain, the USA, the USSR and France led to resentment and tension between the occupying forces and the German population. This was partly because many Germans also regarded themselves as victims of the Second World War, not as perpetrators.

It is estimated that between 1945 and 1947 in the Soviet sector up to two million German women were raped by Soviet soldiers and that approximately 90 per cent of pregnancies in that sector were aborted. This figure does not include the very high number of privately arranged terminations. German men who tried to protect the women were sometimes shot. The high levels of rape continued until better controls were enforced by the USSR on its soldiers in 1947 and harsh penalties were introduced in 1949.

Looting was also very common by the Soviet soldiers in their zone of occupation.

In the Western zones, there was some resentment among German civilians at the lifestyle enjoyed by the occupying forces, especially when Allied soldiers in the Western zones were later joined by their families, and local people were sometimes evicted to provide accommodation. A social club was built for the Western Allies in Berlin, the cost of which could have provided homes for 6000 Germans. The Allied forces and families began to enjoy food levels and accommodation that were in some cases actually better than they would have enjoyed at home. There were reports that these disparities were at their most extreme in the French zone. Segregation policies were also resented, whereby for example, hairdressers had cubicles for Allies and their families and separate ones for Germans, although some Germans acknowledged that this was not so very different to some of the early measures that the Nazis had taken against the Jews. Tensions also rose as war-weary German soldiers and prisoners of war returned home, to discover their wives or partners mixing with American, British and French soldiers. This is shown dramatically in Fassbinder's 1979 feature film *The Marriage of Maria Braun*. These liaisons between the Allied forces and local German women ranged from casual to long term, although US regulations meant that soldiers could not marry German women until both had left Germany. These relationships were also partly prompted by the fact that the presence of large numbers of Allied forces offered commercial sexual opportunities for German women who were financially desperate.

Dealing with shortages

The winter of 1946–7 was extremely severe throughout Germany. There were reports of Germans freezing to death. Three-quarters of industry had to be temporarily shut down because of power shortages. In Hamburg, Germans attacked coal trains in search of fuel and the entire bread rations for the whole of March were used up within little more than a week. Food shortages were more severe in the Western zones because much of Germany's agriculture was in what was now the Soviet zone. Food rationing was implemented, but the rations were considerably lower than wartime levels. Some of the British Army officers administering the occupation of the British zone had to respond to complaints from Britain that they were not being harsh enough on the Germans, especially following the release of film footage showing conditions in the former Nazi concentration camp at Bergen-Belsen. The British occupying forces were able to say with truth that the rations were equivalent to those that prisoners had received in the former Nazi concentration camps. Conditions were so harsh that some Germans believed rumours that the Allies were following a deliberate plan to slowly exterminate the German population. Every scrap of land which could be used for growing food was put to use by ordinary Germans to combat this.

Berliners growing vegetables in front of the destroyed *Reichstag* building in 1946. One of the problems after planting potatoes was to keep starving thieves stealing the seed potatoes out of the ground.

Trümmerfrauen

More than a quarter of Germany's homes and half of its schools had been destroyed during the war. The Allies in all four zones conscripted all German women between the ages of 15 and 50 to clear the huge amounts of rubble. These groups of women were known as the *Trümmerfrauen* (literally 'rubble women') and most of the work was done by hand with chains of women collecting, moving and cleaning the debris from the Allied bombardments in preparation for the rebuilding of German towns and cities. In immediate post-war Germany, there were seven million more women than men. Their demanding and vital work has since been recognised throughout Germany with various memorials and exhibitions.

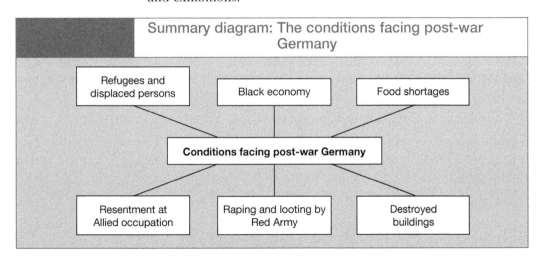

Summary diagram: The conditions facing post-war Germany

- Refugees and displaced persons
- Black economy
- Food shortages

Conditions facing post-war Germany

- Resentment at Allied occupation
- Raping and looting by Red Army
- Destroyed buildings

3 | Denazification

Implementing denazification

The leading members of the former Nazi government had been tried by a tribunal of the four Allied occupying powers at Nuremberg in October 1946. The issue of dealing with other Nazi figures and individuals was clearly going to be much more difficult. Some were in hiding, or had lied to avoid heavy fines or imprisonment. In many instances much of the evidence needed to convict individuals was lost or had deliberately been destroyed. There were also the immense practical difficulties of trying to run a devastated country and put Germany on the path to recovery. Individuals with vital skills such as doctors or teachers were desperately needed to aid Germany's recovery. The policy of denazification proved controversial and difficult to implement. Mary Fulbrook argues that the Western Allies in particular were never really clear about whether they were punishing or rehabilitating Germany, and that denazification by the Western Allies was therefore 'characterised by a degree of confusion and ultimate inefficiency'. There was also a very different ideological stance between the Western Allies and the USSR. The West saw Nazism as the result of the decisions and choices made by individuals. Because of this, their post-war polices emphasised the need for the re-educating of Germans in democratic values. The Soviets, however, interpreted Nazism as a consequence of capitalist social and economic structures and for them denazification was part of an ideologically driven process towards the creation of a socialist society. Denazification was used as a justification for extensive social and economic restructuring in the Soviet zone (page 21).

The inconsistent and sometimes indiscriminate approaches to denazification across the four different sectors caused resentment. This was especially during the initial, more punitive, phase when the Allies were keen on making former *Wehrmacht* soldiers face trial. Many Germans felt that ordinary soldiers had simply been doing their duty and that the Allies did not have a proper understanding of the nature of Nazism. In all four zones, there were cases of former soldiers being arrested, held for more than a year in internment camps, and then suddenly released without any charges having been brought against them. Some managed to escape completely, for example **Josef Mengele** escaped as far away as South America. Others were wrongly arrested, while some managed to secure high-ranking and influential positions in either East or West Germany.

Denazification in the Western zones

The very early stages of denazification proved to be administratively complex and time consuming. The Western Allies required Germans to complete questionnaires, following which individuals were assigned to one of five categories according to the extent of their involvement in Nazism. Individuals who were classified as not having been active

Key question
Why was denazification such a difficult issue?

Key term
Wehrmacht
The German armed forces from 1935 to 1945.

Key figure
Josef Mengele 1911–79
An SS officer and doctor who was infamous for his experiments on prisoners at the Nazi extermination camp at Auschwitz 1943–5. He was never tried for war crimes and died in Brazil in 1979.

Key question
How was denazification carried out in the Western zones?

participants in the Nazi regime collected the so-called 'Persil certificate', a reference to their being 'clean' ('Persil' being the brand name of a popular washing powder). It became increasingly difficult, however, to distinguish between those who may have joined the Nazi Party to keep their jobs and careers, and those who had genuinely been opponents of the Nazi regime. The numbers that claimed always to have been anti-Nazi did seem to the Allies to be rather high.

The process led to a huge backlog of administration and simply became unworkable. The Western Allies soon became more concerned with rebuilding West Germany rather than putting their energies and resources into denazification. By the early 1950s, the whole process had effectively wound down. This led to much criticism both within Germany and internationally, especially when Adenauer's government included several members who had had close associations with the Third Reich government (see page 46). The legal profession in post-war West Germany was later notable for the high proportion of members who had previously been members of the Nazi Party.

Further action against former Nazi war criminals became rather erratic. The first 'Auschwitz trials' were held in Poland in 1947 when Höss, the longest-serving commander of the camp, and five other leading officials from Auschwitz-Birkenau were tried and executed. Höss was actually taken back to Auschwitz-Birkenau to be hanged. A second 'Auschwitz trial' took place in Frankfurt, FRG, between 1963 and 1965. At these second trials, over 200 survivors from Auschwitz-Birkenau were called as witnesses. Seventeen of the 22 on trial received various prison sentences ranging from three years to life imprisonment. These numbers were minimal, when it is remembered that up to 6000 SS members were at some stage involved in the operating of the Auschwitz-Birkenau camp alone.

Since the Second World War, aside from the Nuremberg hearings, there has been the occasional trial of Nazi war criminals and some individuals have been found guilty. Much of this has been the result of efforts of individuals rather than the formal actions of the two German states. Simon Wiesenthal, in particular (who was a Jewish survivor from the Mauthausen concentration camp and who died in 2005), worked tirelessly to track down and bring over 16 individuals to trial during the 1960s. His work, for example, led to the tracing and arrest of **Adolf Eichmann**, who was eventually tried and hanged in Israel in 1962.

Denazification in the Soviet zone

In dealing with individuals, the USSR's process of denazification was much more thorough but also more ruthless in aiming to exclude or remove former Nazis from key positions of influence – such as in government, the legal profession and education. Less thorough denazification procedures were applied to individuals with medical skills, showing that practical necessities sometimes outweighed political considerations.

Key figure

Adolf Eichmann 1906–62
Joined the SS in 1932 and was later in charge of the transportations in Nazi-occupied Poland and Hungary to the extermination camps.

Key question
How was denazification carried out in the Soviet zone?

The denazification process was also used in the Soviet zone to attack individuals who were regarded as being opposed to socialism. Within just three months of its ceasing to be a Nazi concentration camp, Sachsenhausen (on the northern outskirts of Berlin), had become Soviet Special Camp Number 7. Those seen by the USSR as politically unreliable were sent there as well as those Soviet soldiers who had contracted sexually transmitted infections in Soviet-occupied Germany. It became Special Camp Number 1 from 1948 to 1950, during which time approximately 25 per cent of the 60,000 prisoners held there died from malnutrition or disease. Later, from 1950 to 1956, the site was used as a Soviet and GDR army barracks, and in 1961 it was officially made into a memorial by the GDR government for 'anti-fascist freedom fighters'. Soviet Camp Number 2 was established on the site of the former Nazi concentration camp at Buchenwald. It held nearly 30,000 inmates, many of whom were prisoners sentenced for supposedly opposing Soviet rule in the Eastern zone.

Information about the use of these camps by the Soviets for their own political purposes was deliberately censored and did not appear in any history books in the GDR during the period of East Germany's existence. The precise details of these Soviet-run camps were not revealed until 1990. **Helmut Kohl** visited the former Nazi concentration camp at Buchenwald in June 1991 and was the first German Chancellor to commemorate the victims of both the Third Reich and the succeeding GDR government.

Helmut Kohl
Chancellor of the FRG, 1982–90, and Chancellor of reunited Germany, 1990–8.

Key figure

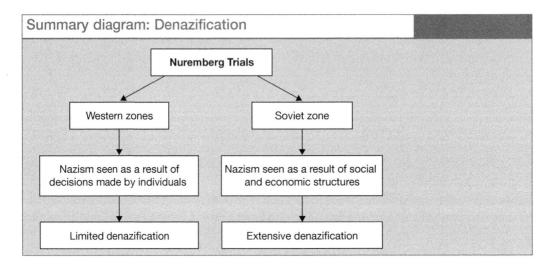

Summary diagram: Denazification

Nuremberg Trials

Western zones → Nazism seen as a result of decisions made by individuals → Limited denazification

Soviet zone → Nazism seen as a result of social and economic structures → Extensive denazification

4 | Developments in Germany 1945–8: The Reasons for Increasing Division

Developments in the Eastern zone

Shortly before end of the war in April 1945, a small group of committed German socialists led by Walter Ulbricht (who always had a Lenin-style beard) arrived in Berlin from exile during the Second World War in the USSR. The previous leader of the German Communist Party, Ernst Thälmann, had been murdered by the Nazis after 12 years' imprisonment in the Buchenwald

Key question
Why did the SED gain control in the Soviet zone?

Ulbricht Group
German communists who had been in exile in the USSR when Hitler was in power. After Germany's surrender, they began developing the Eastern zone along socialist lines under directives from Stalin.

SMAD
The Soviet Military Administration which controlled the USSR's occupation of the Eastern zone.

Stalinist
Ruthless single-party control, as in the USSR.

Anti-Bolshevik
The Bolsheviks, led by Lenin, had taken power in Russia in 1917. Anti-Bolshevism was a fundamental part of Nazi ideology.

concentration camp. At this stage there was no realisation that in just over four years the Eastern zone would be a separate socialist German state firmly allied to the USSR, but the **Ulbricht Group** arrived determined to achieve political power and then to transform German society and economy. They influenced the measures adopted by Soviet Military Administration, **SMAD**, which were designed to achieve, if not the co-operation of the German population, at least the consent or lack of outright opposition.

Democratisation in the Soviet zone

The leaders at Potsdam had agreed that democratisation, the rebirth of political life in Germany, would be one way of denazifying the state. Initially it appeared that SMAD was promoting a form of democracy. The Soviet zone was in fact the first zone which allowed political parties to form. This was a deliberate plan to legitimise the organisation and promotion of the German Communist Party (KPD). Other parties from the Weimar Republic era also resurfaced: the Social Democrats (SPD) and the Liberals (LDP) and a reformed Christian Democrat (CDU) party emerged. Two new political parties were permitted in the Soviet zone to appeal to those unlikely to be reached by the existing political groups: the Democratic Peasants Party (DBD) and the National Democratic Party (NDPD) which was aimed at former Nazis. However, this political activity soon proved to be little more than a sham democracy as the political grip of the Ulbricht group was extended and tightened.

Undoubtedly there was genuine zeal amongst German communists. Even though they were under Soviet control, they were committed to their party's socialist cause. Countless German communists had been killed under Nazism and many of those that had survived had spent many years in hiding, in exile, or were survivors from the Nazi concentration and extermination camps. In the immediate post-war period, the KPD consciously adopted a moderate approach. This was partly because they realised that most Germans needed to use any energy they had just simply to survive – and that they had little time or inclination for discussions on the social and economic transformation of the state. But the control of political life that developed in the ensuing months as Cold War tensions intensified owed much to the **Stalinist** model.

The creation of a ruling SED party

Precisely because of its close links with the USSR, the KPD faced a difficult task in gaining support from the population in the Eastern zone, where there was outrage at the extent of the raping and looting that had accompanied the Soviet Army's occupation. Further, the German population had been fed the **anti-Bolshevik** propaganda of the Third Reich. This meant that the KPD was unable to win much popular support compared to the SPD which remained by far the largest party. There was intense pressure on the SPD during 1945–6 to join the KPD and to form the SED

(Socialist United Party of Germany). In the Soviet zone a formal merger between the SPD and the KPD took place on 22 April 1946. The following day, the SED newspaper **Neues Deutschland** (*New Germany*) was first published. This merger is still subject to debate. During the period of the two Germanys, it was portrayed by most Western historians as being brought about by intimidation by the KPD, whereas in the GDR it was described as a merger by free choice. SMAD did not allow a ballot of SPD members to test acceptance of the merger, and similar merger proposals in the West were rejected by the SPD's membership in the Western sectors of Berlin when a ballot was held. However, some SPD members supported the merger as they felt that valuable lessons from the past needed to be learnt and applied. The failure of the SPD and KPD to co-operate during the Weimar period was widely seen as having allowed the Nazis to become the single largest party in the **Reichstag** in 1932. The merger created a mass party with the political power base which would smooth the implementation of the planned social and economic changes.

Neues Deutschland
The official East German SED newspaper which promoted party policy.

Reichstag
The German Parliament building until 1933 and then again following the reunification of Germany.

Influencing the population

From Hitler Youth to Communist Youth
Young people were strongly urged to become members of the Communist Free German Youth (FDJ). The SED, as the Nazis had done, saw young people as vital to the development of support for the new regime. The FDJ was initially headed by Erich Honecker (see Chapter 4). It was set up in March 1946 for all those aged 14 to 25, although it excluded a small number who had previously been members of the Nazi Party organisations. All other youth organisations apart from church groups were banned to prevent counter-influences. Alan McDougall analyses the experiences of those involved. On the whole, the process seems to have been quite straightforward. By the mid-1940s, many of those in the FDJ would have previously been the very youngest members of the Hitler Youth. The FDJ deliberately avoided organising events such as torch-lit parades. A major appeal, in contrast to the Hitler Youth, was its mixed-sex organisation. It also offered very real educational and recreational activities for many young people in very disadvantaged circumstances. The FDJ was also able to utilise an engrained sense from the Hitler Youth of hard work and individual self-sacrifice in the service of the state. The FDJ was to have problems in later years, when East German society had recovered from the adverse conditions of the immediate post-war period. It then found it difficult to live up to young people's expectations. Even so, as time progressed and the GDR became firmly established, not joining the FDJ often jeopardised young people's educational opportunities and careers.

Mass organisations
Other mass organisations in addition to the FDJ were also set up in the Soviet zone and controlled to help spread the socialist message. These included the Women's Democratic Association,

the Union of those Persecuted by the Nazis, the German Cultural League, and the German–Soviet Friendship Association. By 1947, the vast majority of those living in the Soviet zone were members of at least one organisation under SED control.

Repression of opposition

The ability of the other political parties to constitute any effective opposition was constrained by pressure from SMAD, the dominance of the SED as a political party, its influence over the mass organisations and the imprisonment of those deemed politically unreliable. Many Germans in the Eastern zone soon had the impression that the SED, rather than being a political party, was in fact a tool of the USSR.

The SED's early policies

Key question
What were the key policies of the SED in the years immediately after the Second World War?

Sweeping changes to the society and economy of the Eastern zone were implemented during the period of post-war military government 1945–9. They were driven by socialist principles and by a determination to eradicate Nazism and the factors which had contributed to it. These changes added to the divergence of the Soviet and Western zones of Germany.

Economic changes

Economic reforms were undertaken on socialist principles. They involved the state control of former privately owned banks and the nationalisation of much of industry and commerce – 60 per cent of it by 1949. The most striking measure was the extensive land reform, requiring large landed estates to be redistributed to the state as well as to agricultural labourers and refugees. This land redistribution (under the motto '*Junker* lands into peasants hands') not only reflected socialist principles, it also reduced the power of the group seen to have been influential in the power of Nazism. Although there was widespread opposition to the disruption caused by redistribution, especially from those who had farmed the land in traditional communities for generations, it was greeted with much enthusiasm by thousands of new smallholders. In social terms the balance of power and influence in the Eastern zone was certainly altered. Economically the change was literally counterproductive. The 7000 large estates involved had been more efficient than their smaller replacements were to be.

Education

Sweeping changes to education were also implemented with the aims of:

- removing the aspects which had nurtured Nazism
- creating a more equal society
- implanting socialist values.

In 1946, the Law for the Democratisation of German Schools was implemented. Comprehensive schools replaced the previous selective system for students aged 6–14 years. *Oberschule* provided education for the more able from 14 years of age. The process of

Neue Lehrer für die neue Schule

Bewerbungen für den Beruf des Neulehrers mit ausführlichem Lebenslauf an das Schulwissenschaftliche Institut, Leipzig-53, Gustav Freytag-Str. 42···

An advertisement for 'New teachers for new schools' as part of the denazification process in the Soviet zone, 1946. What message does it seek to convey?

Key figures

Kurt Schumacher 1895–1952
Leader of the West German SPD, 1946–52. He had been badly wounded on the Eastern Front during the First World War. SPD member of the *Reichstag* in 1930. Held in Nazi concentration camps, 1935–45.

Konrad Adenauer 1867–1967
As Mayor of Cologne (1917–33) had refused to allow the city to display swastika flags for a visit by Hitler in 1933. He had also spent two brief periods in Nazi concentration camps in 1934 and 1944.

removing all traces of Nazism from schools created severe shortages of teachers and textbooks initially, but a new centralised curriculum was rapidly introduced with textbooks which were now tailored to socialist rather than Nazi ideals. Students from working-class backgrounds gained new opportunities. The proportion going on to a university education almost doubled in three years. They made up over one-third of university students in 1949. The limitation on opportunity came now not from social background, but from pressure to conform. For example, joining a church congregation or refusal to join the FDJ could result in non-admission to university.

Developments in the Western zones
Political parties

In the Western zones, the Social Democratic Party (SPD) under **Kurt Schumacher** and the German Communist Party (KPD) quickly re-established themselves but they were opposed to any merger. The various Christian and conservative parties (including the old Catholic Centre Party) joined together to form the non-denominational Christian Democratic Union (CDU) led by **Konrad Adenauer** (see pages 44–5) and the Christian Social Union (CSU) in Bavaria. This merger of Catholics and Protestants into one political party was a deliberate attempt to work together and prevent the fragmentation of the political

Key question
What political parties emerged in the Western zones?

parties which had had occurred during the Weimar Republic. The various liberal parties formed the Free Democratic Party (FDP). There were a number of other smaller political parties, such as the League of Expellees and Refugees (BHE). There were no corresponding attempts in the Western zones at radical social and economic change such as had been initiated in the Eastern zone with its land reforms and the mass organisations. The main political divide between the two major parties in the west (the SPD and the CDU/CSU) was their different views on the fate of the Western zones and how far to ally themselves with the Western Allies (see pages 30 and 45).

The Truman Doctrine

The increasing distrust between East and West over issues in Germany must also be seen against the wider international background of growing suspicion and tensions between the Western Allies and the USSR from 1945. This was to lead to what we now refer to as the Cold War. In March 1946, Churchill made his 'Iron Curtain' speech and he urged the development of a Western alliance as a defence against the spread of socialism. At this time there were also fears in the West that the communists might succeed in the **Greek Civil War**. The USA made clear its views on the threat of the spread of communism. The Truman Doctrine stated that the USA was firmly intent on containing communism throughout the world.

The Marshall Plan

The USA then announced the Marshall Plan in the summer of 1947. It was partly a response to the setting up by Stalin of **COMINFORM**, which was an organisation to co-ordinate the policies and strategies of the various socialist political parties throughout the Eastern bloc. These socialist parties would then work together in ideological unity to develop economic and social systems based on the Soviet model.

The Marshall Plan aimed to prevent the spread of communism by reviving the European economy. It also aimed to expand the market for US goods. In the case of Germany it also represented a significant change in US policy from punishing to rebuilding Germany. It reflected a recognition that a strong Germany with a rebuilt economy could act as a defence against communist expansion. The plan was famously denounced by V. Molotov, the Soviet foreign minister, as 'dollar imperialism'. Stalin strictly forbade any Eastern European state to accept Marshall Aid.

Within four years, US$13,000 billion were taken up by the majority of Western nations and the Western zone of Germany. Over the next two years much of Western Europe saw unprecedented economic growth and the degree of popular support for communist parties fell dramatically in the areas receiving Marshall Aid. Aid was administered through the OEEC (the Organisation for European Economic Co-operation). Participation in a common organisation promoted closer working between the administrators of the Western zones of Germany. The OEEC also

Key dates

Truman Doctrine announced: March 1947

US government announced the Marshall Plan: July 1947

Key terms

Greek Civil War Following occupation by Nazi Germany there was a civil war, 1946–9, between the government and communist forces.

COMINFORM The Communist Information Bureau. Set up in 1947 by the USSR to organise communist infiltration and intelligence gathering in non-communist states.

laid the foundations for later Western European integration. Stalin responded to the Marshall Plan with **COMECON**, although this organisation would prove unable to provide the levels of financial aid to the Eastern bloc which the USA could offer to Western Europe. Politically, the Marshall Plan had the effect of increasing the division between the Western zones and the East.

COMECON
The economic organisation of the Eastern bloc and the USSR, set up in 1949.

Bizonia

In January 1947 the British and Americans merged their zones to create Bizonia in order to administer aspects of the economy more efficiently. It certainly aided German economic recovery, but it was a step which would make the reuniting of Germany much less likely. A London conference in late 1947 ended with hostility between the USSR and the Western powers. The USSR argued that Bizonia was in breach of agreements made at the Potsdam Conference, while Britain and the USA opposed Stalin's proposal for a united, neutral Germany. The Western Allies feared that this would become entirely socialist.

Key dates

Formation of Bizonia: January 1947

Currency reform in the Western zones: June 1948

Berlin Blockade and Berlin Airlift started: June 1948

Currency reform

In June 1948 the *Deutschmark* (DM) was introduced into the three Western zones, an indication of their even closer co-operation. The previous currency had lost almost all its value partly because of the excessive printing of money by the Soviets. Bartering had replaced the *Reichsmark* (RM) for most transactions. The currency reform was vital if the German economy was to revive: trade cannot prosper if currency is not trusted. However, this currency reform increased the economic divergence between the Western and Soviet zones. The USSR also introduced a new currency in their zone. In the Soviet zone the increasing divide was met with intense propaganda, claiming that the USA was using thousands of Germans for slave labour, that thousands were leaving the Western zones for the east, and that the Western powers were preparing to abandon West Berlin. It also meant that the Western and Soviet zones were developing into two very different political and economic systems.

Key question
How did the currency reform affect Germany?

The Berlin Blockade and its impact

The Soviets responded to currency reform in the Western zones with the Berlin Blockade from June 1948 to May 1949. This imposed a blockade of all land and water routes between the Western zones and West Berlin. The Berlin Blockade seems not to have been a sudden decision. Since the setting up of Bizonia, the USSR had increasingly obstructed access routes to West Berlin. Barriers would suddenly appear and disappear on roads, canals were sometimes blocked, trains from the west would be diverted, and the Western Allies' soldiers were increasingly subjected to identity checks by Soviet soldiers. Access routes to West Berlin had become so restricted by the Soviets that the Western Allies had already begun supplying their troops in West Berlin by air. The full blockade meant that the entire civilian population now had to be supplied by air. Stalin's aim for the blockade was to

Key question
What was the significance of the Berlin Blockade and the Berlin Airlift?

force the Western Allies to relinquish their zones in Berlin. West Berlin would then join East Berlin as one integrated city under Soviet control.

The Western powers, mainly under the urging of US General Clay, launched the Berlin Airlift, which lasted for 11 months. West Berlin's population of two million was supplied with food and fuel entirely by air. Initially this looked a daunting, if not, impossible, task. At its height, an aircraft was landing with food and fuel supplies at **Tempelhof Airport** in West Berlin every 90 seconds.

West Berlin had suddenly been transformed from being a symbol of the Nazi dictatorship to a city where Western, democratic values needed to be protected by the Western Allies. The Berlin Airlift, therefore, had a significant psychological impact. It symbolised the defence of the West against the East and allayed the fears of many West Berliners that they were eventually going to be abandoned by the Western powers. It is ironic that the Soviets clearly intended that their blockade would force the West to surrender West Berlin. Previously, some US politicians had talked of withdrawing from West Berlin. Instead, the Soviet blockade had turned West Berlin into a crusade for the Western Allies. The American public responded by sending nearly five million packages to Germany, which included food, coffee and clothes. Eventually, after 11 months, the USSR called off the blockade.

The Berlin Airlift made the division of Germany and the creation of a united Western zone almost inevitable. Following the Berlin Airlift, the Western powers decided to co-ordinate their armed forces and this laid the early foundations for NATO – a development to which Stalin would soon have to respond. The

Key term

Tempelhof Airport
A commercial airport until October 2008. On its final day of operation elderly Berliners held placards stating 'Thank you America'.

Key date

Berlin Blockade and Berlin Airlift ended: May 1949

Children in West Berlin waving at US aeroplanes making deliveries during the Berlin Blockade, 1948.

airlift had been carried out with impressive logistical planning and succeeded when many believed it would fail. Today, there is a memorial at the site for the 48 British and US pilots who died in the airlift. The airlift itself is still often portrayed in Cold War imagery with the Soviet as aggressor and the USA as liberator. In the long term, the evacuation of the entire population of West Berlin might have provided the West with easier-to-defend boundaries, but it was not an option, given the iconic status of Berlin. The Western powers regarded its loss as unthinkable. The Berlin Blockade also helped to increase support in the Western zones for Adenauer's policy of their rapid integration with the Western Allies.

The consolidation of Germany's division by 1949

By 1948 both the Soviet and Western zones of Germany were becoming politically, socially and economically more like their respective occupying powers. In the context of the growing international suspicion and distrust, two distinct Germanys were emerging without any direct reference to the German people themselves. Their destiny was being played out against the background of US–Soviet rivalry. Indeed, it could be said that it was not until the end of the Cold War that the historical circumstances existed in which Germany could be reunited (see Chapters 4 and 5). By June 1948, within a matter of days of the beginning of the airlift, the USA and Britain had agreed to the setting up of a West German state. The Berlin Airlift was therefore a significant factor in accelerating the division of Germany. The French added their zone in April 1949 to form Trizonia, while Stalin made repeated requests for all Allied troops to withdraw to allow for a reunited, neutral Germany.

Progress on demilitarisation, denazification, democratisation and decartelisation

The Allies at Potsdam had agreed that four elements would shape their handling of the administration of their zones in the immediate post-war era: demilitarisation, denazification, democratisation and **decartelisation** – the 'four Ds'. Demilitarisation was fully implemented (see page 7). Progress in the other three Ds demonstrates the different values and priorities of the Western Allies compared to the USSR.

By 1949 in the West, the push to denazify had given way to the higher priority of making use of professional expertise and achieving efficiency to ensure economic growth. Decartelisation had resulted in only a limited restructuring of large business and financial organisations and the application of the principle of co-determination was limited to key industries (page 44). However, democratic activity was beginning to resurface.

In the Soviet zone so-called democratisation was developing along Stalinist lines with a one-party state which was reminiscent of Nazi government. The other two Ds, which were social and economic in nature, were much more thoroughly and systematically addressed.

Key question
How effectively did the Allies apply each of the 'four Ds' to immediate post-war Germany?

Key term

Decartelisation
The reduction in the power and influence of big business interests that had supported the Nazi government.

Summary diagram: Developments in Germany 1945–9 – the reasons for increasing division

```
                    ┌─────────────────────────────────┐
                    │  Reasons for increasing division │
                    └─────────────────────────────────┘
                              │
              ┌───────────────┴───────────────┐
           West                             East
```

West	East
Truman Doctrine Marshall Plan Currency reform	Radical political, social and economic changes
Berlin airlift Formation of FRG Adenauer as Chancellor	COMECON The *Ostmark* Berlin Blockade
	Formation of GDR

Key question
What were the key features of the FRG's constitution?

Key dates

Formation of the FRG: May 1949

Adenauer became the first Chancellor of the FRG: August 1949

Key term

Basic Law
The constitution of the newly formed FRG.

5 | The Establishment of Two German States in 1949

The formation of the FRG

The FRG was set up in May 1949 under the **Basic Law** which set out a temporary West German constitution. This was seen as a temporary arrangement, which would later be replaced by a constitution that would cover a reunited Germany. The FRG's foreign affairs were dealt with by an Allied High Commission until 1951 when West Germany gained its own foreign minister. The Basic Law established a federal state and put in place constitutional controls to prevent some of the conditions which had contributed to the democratic fragility and eventual collapse of the Weimar Republic. Chiefly these were:

- The President could not remove the Chancellor.
- Political parties were required to secure a minimum of five per cent of the vote to enter either federal or state parliaments. This was to prevent the entry of extreme political parties into both local and national politics.

In the Western zones the first federal elections took place in August 1949, which the CDU/CSU won with a narrow margin of 139 seats over the SPD with 131 seats. Konrad Adenauer, leader of the CDU, became the first Chancellor of the FRG and Theodor Heuss (FDP) became the first President. The stability of the new West German government would depend on the continued support from the liberals, the FDP. There were some concerns and fears, both within the FRG and abroad, that there might be a repeat of the weak coalition governments that had undermined the Weimar Republic. Schumacher, as leader of the SPD, also believed that Adenauer would soon become a puppet of the USA and that public opinion would soon turn against him. The FRG formally came into existence in September 1949 and Bonn was chosen as West Germany's capital, but this was seen as provisional and Germany's division was viewed as temporary.

The tasks facing Adenauer were immense. There was a 'new' nation to be built from the trauma and ruins of the Third Reich and the Second World War, a continued refugee crisis, rising prices, and a very uneasy relationship with foreign powers. The existence of 'another Germany' also presented a real dilemma. But Adenauer had campaigned on the premise that economic growth was dependent on the merger of the three Western zones, even if this meant sacrificing 'the fourth' zone to the USSR. This was very controversial and Adenauer was seen by some as being prepared to leave the Germans in the east to the fate of the USSR, while prematurely allying the FRG firmly with the West. Schumacher even went so far as to call him a traitor to the German people. The SPD were less keen for Germany's fate to be tied to the USA and even campaigned for Germany to return to its pre-First World War role, when it had been seen as a balance between Western Europe and the former Russian Empire.

The formation of the GDR

The USSR responded in October 1949 by making its zone the GDR. Pieck was appointed President, Grotewohl Prime Minister and Ulbricht became First Secretary of the **Politburo**. However, as

Key question
Why did so much power lie with the SED?

Politburo
The most senior executive and policy-making committee in the SED ruling government in East Germany.

Key term

'The Ballast', 1949. This cartoon by Kurt Poltiniak, an East German, shows Adenauer and Heuss throwing out the common interests of Germany in order to make the balloon rise.

Formation of the
GDR: October 1949

the SED was the dominant party, political power and decision-making really lay with the SED First Secretary rather than with the President or Prime Minister. Constitutionally, there was freedom of speech, the right to strike, freedom of assembly and freedom to practise religion. In practice, the situation became very different as freedoms were subordinated to Ulbricht's 'building of socialism' and the development of a socialist state closely allied to the USSR.

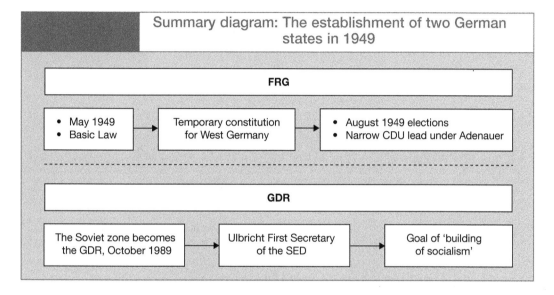

Summary diagram: The establishment of two German states in 1949

FRG

- May 1949
- Basic Law

→ Temporary constitution for West Germany →

- August 1949 elections
- Narrow CDU lead under Adenauer

GDR

The Soviet zone becomes the GDR, October 1989 → Ulbricht First Secretary of the SED → Goal of 'building of socialism'

6 | The Key Debate

Why did Germany become divided in 1949?

This immediate post-war period saw a transition from the chaos that defeated Germany found itself in 1945 to the formal establishment of two separate German states in 1949. In the early post-war period, many Germans hoped for a new beginning in German history – visions of a 'Third Way' – a democratic socialism between Stalinist communism and conservative capitalism. Many hoped for a united, neutral, non-militarised Germany. At this stage, it was by no means clear that either the FRG or the GDR would emerge as separate successful states. Even after the formal division, many Germans hoped that their country would soon be reunited. Why did the Allied occupation end in the formal division of Germany, a development that, initially, had not been intended by either side? Were the seeds of eventual separation already there in the Potsdam Conference in July 1945? Were distinct opportunities missed for Germany to remain as a single nation? What role did Cold War rivalries play? Did they mean that Germany's fortunes became so bound up in the global climate that it left Germany itself with no room to manoeuvre?

Debates on the eventual partition of Germany by 1949

At the Potsdam Conference the permanent division of Germany was never intended by the Allies. Opinions vary as to:

- where responsibility for the division of Germany lay
- at what point the division of Germany became apparent
- whether the formal division of Germany into west and east in 1949 remained open for negotiation, at least until Stalin's 'note' of 1952 (see Chapter 2, page 40).

Following the Potsdam Conference tensions and divisions grew between the USSR and the Western Allies. Traditional Cold War accounts in the West portrayed the USSR as pursuing policies to expand socialist control in Eastern Europe. The Western Allies were portrayed as defensive freedom fighters having to respond to Stalin with strong military and economic policies to combat the spread of socialism.

However, revisionist historians have painted a more complex picture. It is suggested that the USSR was primarily reacting to the initiatives of the Western Allies; the Truman Doctrine, Marshall Plan and the currency reform in their zones. Further, the extent to which Stalin actually wanted the GDR as part of Soviet control of Eastern Europe is debated. Soviet leaders themselves had opinions that ranged from regarding the GDR as a vital part of the Eastern bloc, containing valuable raw materials such as uranium, to seeing it as a drain on hard-pressed Soviet economic and military resources. Historians such as Wilfried Loth have argued that Stalin really would have preferred a neutral, reunited Germany, and that the USSR ended up with 'exactly what he sought to avoid'.

The decisions of German politicians in both zones also played a part. Influential figures in the West advocated rapid alliance with the Western powers. Adenauer was impatient for Germany's Western zones to ally with the Western Allies (see page 48). Opinions on Adenauer's intentions differ. It is debated whether he intended to pursue the reuniting of Germany once the FRG was economically and militarily strong enough, or whether he was simply willing to leave the Eastern zone to the USSR. Revisionist accounts also question the extent to which socialism was thrust on to an unwilling German population in the East. Gareth Pritchard argues that the establishment of socialism in GDR was a product of committed German socialists and their desire to create an anti-Nazi state. Mark Allinson argues that while some East Germans tolerated the establishment of socialism in the Soviet zone, others genuinely believed in co-operation with the USSR to create a new socialist society.

Some key books in the debate

M. Allinson, *Politics and Popular Opinion in East Germany* (Manchester, 2000)
W. Loth, *Stalin's Unwanted Children* (Palgrave, 1998)
G. Pritchard, *The Making of the GDR 1945–53* (Manchester, 2000)

Study Guide: AS Question

In the style of Edexcel

How far do you agree that the actions of the USSR were primarily responsible for the division of Germany in 1949?

Exam tips

The cross-references are intended to take you straight to the material that will help you to answer the question.

This question is asking you to explain and evaluate the causes of Germany's division. The key words to think about when planning your answer to this question are 'actions of the USSR' and 'primarily responsible'.

You will need to be clear about the way in which Stalin's policies contributed to the division, but the word 'mainly' implies that you will need to show the contribution of other factors, too.

You should plan to devote a third to a half of your answer to 'actions of the USSR', allowing yourself time to deal convincingly with other factors, for example, the decisions of the Western Allies and the context of the developing Cold War which also played their part in the division of Germany into two states. There is no need to prove a narrative of events, but you should show how actions by one side provoked reactions by the other.

In support of the argument that actions of the USSR were significant you could show:

- Stalin's determination to create a buffer zone for the future protection of the USSR, and the breakdown of wartime co-operation as a result of Soviet encroachment in Eastern Europe (pages 8–10).
- Stalin's introduction of communist-style government in the Soviet zone and in other areas occupied by the Soviet army, which alarmed the USA in particular (pages 18–22).
- Stalin's decision to impose the Berlin Blockade which led directly to the heightening of Cold War tensions, the creation of NATO, and the decision to create the FRG (pages 24–6).

In support of the significance of other factors you could show that:

- The events in Germany were influenced by the wider context of Cold War rivalry. There is much debate about the origins and responsibility for this (page 30).
- The Truman Doctrine and the Marshall Plan – themselves a reaction to the threat of communist expansion – intensified Cold War divisions (page 23).
- The British and Americans' establishment of Bizonia was interpreted by Stalin as an initiative designed to create a separate political body and as an anti-Soviet move (page 24).
- Stalin's proposal for a German government was rejected at the London Conference of 1947 because of fears of the spread of communism (page 24).

- The currency reform created a separate economic entity in the West (page 24).
- Adenauer's preference for Western integration was influential (page 30).

You should round off your answer by offering your judgement: do you agree with the statement in the question? The Cold War influence on the division of Germany was so strong that you should take this into account when coming to a judgement.

Study Guide: A2 Question

In the style of AQA

How successfully, by the mid-1950s, had the policy of denazification, as agreed at the Potsdam Conference, been carried out in Germany?

Exam tips

The cross-references are intended to take you straight to the material that will help you to answer the question.

In order to answer this question you will need to re-read the section on the Potsdam Conference (page 7) in order to explain the intention of denazification (pages 7–8), the Nuremberg Trials and the process of denazification (pages 16–18 and 26). This should enable you to comment on the implementation and success of the policy. Do not forget that you will need to address both the FRG and the GDR and you would be advised to provide some explanatory comment relating to the differences in approach.

You will need to assess:

- The stringency of the Nuremberg Trials.
- The degree to which former Nazis were removed from influential positions in the East and the West.
- The problems encountered in carrying through denazification.

You will need to provide an overall conclusion in which you show a personal judgement and some comparative comment.

---

2 Contrasting Economic and Political Development of FRG and GDR c1950–70

POINTS TO CONSIDER

For many Germans the immediate post-war years had been arguably more traumatic than the Second World War itself. The period from 1945 to the mid-1960s, however, saw two very different Germanys emerging from their very precarious beginnings. In many ways both Germanys became two politically and economically successful states with two very contrasting ideological systems.

The period is also one of an uneasy relationship between the FRG and GDR. While Cold War rivalries and distrust meant that there was outright hostility and propaganda campaigns between the two Germanys, there was a formal commitment in West Germany's constitution to reunification and many Germans suffered as a result of the loss of family and friends in the 'other Germany'. Undoubtedly the most significant and symbolic single event in Germany's post-war history was the building of the Berlin Wall in 1961.

The major themes covered are:

- The beginnings of divergence between the FRG and the GDR
- Developments in the FRG under Adenauer
- Developments in the GDR under Ulbricht 1950–71
- Emigration from the GDR to the FRG and the building of the Berlin Wall in 1961

Key dates

1950		Start of the Korean War
1951		Signing of the European Coal and Steel (ECSC) Treaty in Paris
1952		The 'Stalin note'
1953		Death of Stalin
		June uprising in the GDR
1955		FRG became an independent state
		FRG and GDR joined NATO and the Warsaw Pact, respectively.
		Compulsory military service began in the FRG
1961	August 13	Construction of the Berlin Wall began

1962	Compulsory military service began in the GDR
	The *Spiegel* affair
1963	Adenauer resigned and was succeeded by Erhard
1966	Formation of the 'Grand Coalition' between the CDU/CSU and the SPD in the FRG

1 | The Beginnings of Divergence Between the FRG and the GDR

Key question
To what extent did the FRG and GDR become models of their respective ideological systems?

Key developments in both Germanys

From the 1950s to the mid-1960s, West German federal government was dominated by the CDU/CSU (see pages 44–51) led by Adenauer until 1963 and then by Erhard to 1966. It was a time of impressive economic growth and the continued political and economic integration of the FRG with Western Europe and the USA. However, this period also saw growing criticism of the FRG as a materialistic, self-satisfied and politically conservative society.

In the GDR, this period saw the creation of a highly disciplined socialist government controlled by the SED, and its full integration with the Eastern bloc and the USSR. The GDR did achieve some economic and social improvements, especially when compared with the other Eastern bloc states, but this has to be weighed against the increase in state repression and control. As you study developments in the GDR you should consider whether it was simply a dictatorship imposing its will on the East German people or whether there was some genuine popular support for the ruling SED and its policies (see also Chapter 4, page 115).

Both states had very uncertain and shaky beginnings and were heavily burdened with the legacies of the Second World War, the aftermath of the Holocaust and the effects of Allied occupation. Although many Germans in the initial post-war period sought a political and economic structure that lay somewhere between Stalinism and Western capitalism (a 'Third Way'), both Germanys eventually became very successful, if not model, examples of their respective ideological systems. The FRG soon became a sound democracy with a robust economy that was envied by many other Western states. Similarly, the GDR was widely regarded as the most successful Eastern bloc state – in terms of both its economy and the lack of widespread dissent between 1953 and 1988. Table 2.1 (see page 36) summarises the key economic and political developments of both the FRG and the GDR.

Assessments of the successes of both Germanys

Although historians have been impressed by the economic performance of the FRG, some have challenged its claims to be a full democracy. Otto Kirchheimer, for instance, described the limited difference in policies between the SPD and CDU/CSU for

Table 2.1: A summary of the key economic and political developments in the FRG and the GDR

	FRG	GDR
Economic success	The FRG witnessed what became widely known as the 'economic miracle'. It was run on **'social-market'** economic principles and the results were envied by many other Western states. It became a founding member of the **EEC**.	The GDR was generally seen as the most successful socialist state in the Eastern bloc. By the late 1960s, it had higher standards of living than any of the other neighbouring socialist states. By 1964, the USSR claimed that the GDR was one of the strongest states in the whole of Europe. It became a member of the Eastern bloc COMECON.
Political stability	The FRG developed into a very successful, well-functioning democracy, which is not what many would have predicted when it was formed in 1949. After the failures of Weimar democracy and the Third Reich dictatorship many feared that most West Germans would not successfully adapt to democracy.	An uprising in June 1953 was successfully repressed by the GDR government with support from the USSR. It was then not until 1989 that there was any widespread threat to the government. There was no need for Soviet intervention to maintain the government's authority – unlike in Hungary (1956) and in Czechoslovakia (1968).

the FRG electorate as a 'vanishing opposition'. This in effect, limited the democratic choices available to the electorate. Similarly, the GDR's claims to be a 'classless society' have been challenged. There were clear inequalities in the GDR, which included the relative luxurious lifestyle enjoyed by members of the Politburo, the denial of university places to those from more 'bourgeois' backgrounds, and the lack of advancement for women in certain professions.

The two Germanys' portrayal of each other

The FRG and GDR dealt with the recent past in very contrasting ways and it is very difficult to gauge where the Germans' sense of national identity lay. Both the GDR and the FRG also had to come to terms with the irony that they had rapidly become firm allies of their former enemies. Further, the rearmament of both Germanys in the mid-1950s was met with much internal opposition in both the FRG and the GDR. Many who had friends and family in the 'other Germany' felt significant unease that their respective armed forces would soon be facing each other.

Throughout the Cold War both German governments carried out media and propaganda campaigns against the other, while simultaneously many ordinary Germans wanted reunification for personal reasons. The GDR stressed its work towards developing an egalitarian, socialist society, and therefore emphasised the economic inequalities and social problems in the FRG: homelessness, drugs and unemployment. The FRG stressed its political freedoms and respect for human rights and criticised the GDR for its totalitarianism, state-led oppression and the lack of

Key question
How did the two Germanys view each other?

Social market
The combination of free, capitalist markets and the state's protection of workers' rights and welfare.

EEC
European Economic Community – the forerunner of today's European Union.

Key terms

personal freedoms – especially the right to free opinion and the right to travel. Each 'Germany' denounced the other as a historical continuation of the Third Reich. The FRG argued that the GDR was a continuation of a dictatorship from Nazism to the SED-controlled state, whereas the GDR claimed it was the 'only Germany' that was genuinely 'anti-fascist'. Table 2.2 summaries the key political systems in the FRG and the GDR.

The propaganda war was always going to problematic for the GDR. One of the main reasons was that East German citizens could receive West German television and radio broadcasts. Although watching and listening to these was actually illegal in the GDR until 1974, it was virtually impossible for the East German authorities to enforce the ban. West German television and radio significantly undermined the GDR government's propaganda messages. A standing joke in the GDR about the 'dumb Dresden people' who lived in an area of the GDR that could not receive West German television was evidence of a prevailing scepticism within the GDR. It shows how the government's political statements and propaganda were seen by many of the East German public. Konrad Jarausch observes, 'every evening East Germans gathered in front of television sets to emigrate to the West for a few hours without actually leaving their homes'.

At the same time, both German governments had a population that suffered huge losses of family and friendship ties when Germany was divided. This division was brutally reinforced with the building of the Berlin Wall in 1961 and the extensive fortifications along the 'inner-German border'. The euphoria with which many Germans on both sides of the border celebrated the opening of the Berlin Wall in November 1989 also indicates that the Germans had retained their sense of national identity as a unified state – and suggests that Germany's division was largely

Table 2.2: The key features of the political systems of the FRG and the GDR

The political system in the FRG	The political system in the GDR
1. Federal states (*Länder*) had significant responsibilities and power.	1. A federal state, although the five historical *Länder* were later replaced by smaller *Bezirke* run from East Berlin.
2. A formal Head of State with a President with ceremonial and largely symbolic role.	2. A formal Head of State with a President with a ceremonial and largely symbolic role. The role of President was taken over by the Council of State when Pieck died in 1960.
3. Two chambers or houses of parliament. The members of the main law-making chamber, the *Bundestag*, members were elected. The *Bundesrat* membership was made up of representatives sent from each region of the FRG.	3. Two chambers or houses of parliament. The *Volkskammer* was the elected national assembly, but with a predetermined majority of seats for the SED. The *Länderkammer*'s membership was made up of representatives sent from each region of the GDR.
4. Elections were by a complex system of proportional representation with a later clause adding that any political party with less than five per cent of the vote could not take seats in parliament. Political parties which did not support democratic principles could be banned.	4. The main political force was the General Secretary of the SED who increasingly controlled the other political parties and the mass state organisations.

determined by the relations between the superpowers and their respective allies (see Chapter 4 and 5).

The treatment of Jews in the two Germanys

Relations between post-war Germany and the surviving Jewish populations and with the newly established state of Israel were very sensitive. There were also incidents of major embarrassment for the FRG. For example, in 1958 the newly reopened synagogue in Cologne, which had been destroyed in 1938 during **Kristallnacht**, was daubed with 'Jews Out' graffiti and swastikas. It took two weeks before Adenauer officially denounced this act on West German television and radio. Adenauer himself was particularly anxious over international reactions to Germany during Eichmann's trial in Jerusalem in 1961.

The Holocaust and Germany's post-war Jewish survivors were dealt with very differently by the two post-war Germanys as shown in Table 2.3.

Key question
How were Jewish Holocaust survivors treated differently in the two Germanys?

Kristallnacht
The destruction during the Third Reich of many Jewish businesses, synagogues and homes throughout Germany on 9 November 1938.

Key term

Table 2.3: A summary of the treatment of former Nazi concentration camps and Jewish survivors by the FRG and GDR

FRG	GDR
Those former Nazi concentration camps which were preserved as memorial sites within the FRG emphasised the extent of anti-Semitic persecution under Nazism.	Those former Nazi concentration camps which were preserved within the GDR were presented as memorials to 'anti-fascist freedom fighters'. They emphasised the persecution of communists under Nazism.
A scheme of compensation payments was set up for Jewish survivors of the Holocaust (such payments were not made to gypsies or homosexual survivors who had been persecuted during the Third Reich). The FRG also made payments of nearly DM8 million to Czechoslovakia in 1969 to the victims of Nazi concentration camp experiments, and over DM100 million to Hungary in 1971 to victims of Nazism.	The GDR did give Jews an additional pension allowance but it was less than that received by those classified as 'fascist-resistance fighters'.

Key question
How did the two Germanys develop different relationships with the Middle East?

The two Germanys' relationships with Israel and the Middle East

Box 2.1 below shows the contrasting relationships that began to develop between the two Germanys and the Middle East.

Box 2.1: The contrasting relationships between the FRG and the GDR and the Middle East

FRG	GDR
The FRG and Israel established full democratic relations in 1965. However, it did mean cancelling arms sales from the FRG to Arab states and the end of diplomatic relations between the FRG and most states in the Middle East. Previously, the FRG had supported Egypt financially and West German scientists had helped Egypt's rocket programme. This change of policy was challenged by West German industrialists and some members of the government, and met public opposition.	Initially the GDR welcomed Israel as a socialist state, but it soon regarded Israel as an imperial, Middle-Eastern power. The GDR began supporting Arab and Palestinian groups and Ulbricht's state visit to Egypt alarmed the West German government. The GDR government mocked the development of FRG–Israeli relations.

Key term

Hard currency
A currency that the market considers to be strong because its value does not fall, in this case the *Deutschemark*.

Table 2.4: Inter-German trade turnover (in *Reichsmark*) 1960–85

1960	1,600
1965	1,800
1970	3,400
1975	4,900
1980	7,300
1985	11,400

Trade between the two Germanys

Although they characterised each other politically as enemies, the two Germanys entered into mutually beneficial trading agreements. 'Inter-German trade' between the FRG and GDR was categorised as domestic trade and so did not incur any tariffs or taxes; in an economic sense, the GDR was actually an unofficial part of the EEC which the FRG joined as a founder member in 1951. After the building of the Berlin Wall the GDR also benefited from the **hard currency** which all Western visitors had to pay on entering the GDR. Table 2.4 shows the growth of trade between the two Germanys.

The Hallstein Doctrine

Key question
What impact did the Hallstein Doctrine have on relations between the FRG and GDR?

It must be remembered that the FRG's constitution was formally committed to the reunification of Germany – a commitment which the GDR argued was imperialist and counter-revolutionary. This principle was known as the Hallstein Doctrine and was a key principle of the FRG's post-war foreign policy. It was strongly supported by the West German CDU/CSU, which remained firmly committed to German reunification. It was also keenly supported by those Germans who had been forcibly expelled from Germany's former territories in the east at the end of the Second World War. The doctrine stated that the FRG had the right to represent the entire German nation and that the FRG would not maintain any diplomatic relations with any nation that recognised the GDR, with the exception of the USSR. Any establishment of diplomatic relations by another state with the GDR was considered by the West German government as an unfriendly act.

This doctrine challenged the legitimacy of GDR, referring to it as 'a zone' and not a state. What were the implications of the Hallstein Doctrine? It supported and represented the rights of all Germans to be regarded as one people. But its hard-line stance in practice actually helped to sustain Germany's division and deepen the gulf between them. It was not until 1972 that the two Germanys formally recognised each other with the development of Brandt's **Ostpolitik** which recognised the FRG and GDR as two separate states, but not as two independent nations (see pages 75–7). The legacy of the Second World War also meant that it took the GDR a long time to be accepted by other Eastern bloc states. Poland and Czechoslovakia in particular, viewed the GDR as a means of keeping Germany divided, rather than respecting it as a separate state.

William Gray argues that the Hallstein Doctrine was deliberately pursued by the FRG to isolate the GDR internationally. In practice this meant that any offers, such as financial assistance, technical or military expertise by the GDR to developing countries around the world frequently produced more generous counter-offers from the FRG. This meant West German ambassadors travelled to far-flung and often remote parts of the world to try and undermine the GDR's attempts to develop relationships with countries in Africa, Asia, Central and South America. This even led to the developing countries sometimes playing the FRG and GDR off against the other in order to secure the best deals.

Ostpolitik
'Eastern policy':
an attempt to
normalise relations
between West
Germany and the
Eastern Bloc.

Policy of strength
A policy especially
associated with
Adenauer. It sought
to increase the
FRG's military and
economic strength
in order to put
them in a stronger
position to counter
socialism.

Key terms

Was there a missed opportunity for the reuniting of Germany in 1952?

In March 1952, the Western Allies received a 'note' from Stalin that proposed reuniting the four occupation zones of Germany. This note argued for a neutral, disarmed Germany within the borders which had been agreed at Potsdam. It also proposed that Germany would have the right to a multi-party political system with elections overseen by the four occupying powers. However, the Western Allies rejected the Oder–Neisse line as Germany's eastern border and were against elections being monitored by the occupying powers. The Western Allies preferred to pursue a '**policy of strength**' towards the GDR and the USSR. This 1952 'Stalin note' has received various interpretations and a debate about whether it offered a genuine opportunity for reuniting Germany in 1952.

Table 2.5 shows a summary of the various opinions regarding the 1952 'missed opportunity'.

Key question
Could Germany have
been reunited by the
early 1950s?

The 'Stalin note':
1952

Key date

Table 2.5: A summary of the various opinions on the 'Stalin note'

Differing views of Stalin's motives	*Differing views of Adenauer's attitude to the 'note'*
1. Stalin genuinely wanted the setting up of a neutral, reunited Germany. The GDR was a burden on Soviet resources, and by 1952 Stalin had drained the zone of reparations. In the GDR, Ulbricht promoted the note as the creation of a 'peaceful, central European bloc'. 2. If he succeeded in achieving a neutral united Germany, Stalin could then try to expand Soviet influence over all of Germany and even further into Western Europe. 3. Stalin wanted any negotiations with the West to fail. He could then justify proceeding with fully integrating the GDR into the Eastern bloc. The GDR was economically and militarily beneficial to the USSR and the GDR leadership was committed to socialism.	1. Adenauer viewed the 'note' as a deliberate attempt to undermine the FRG's relations with the Western Allies. He maintained that the circumstances for German reunification would be possible only when the FRG was firmly established and a strong power in its own right. Adenauer claimed that he did not see Germany's division as permanent. This became known as 'magnet theory' with the belief that a strong FRG would act as a pull for those in the GDR and would therefore undermine socialism. 2. Adenauer felt that a reunited, neutral Germany would be unable to defend itself against further Soviet expansion westwards. 3. In reality, Adenauer had very little influence and the FRG's increasing westward alignment was mainly due to the Western Allies and the onset of the Cold War.

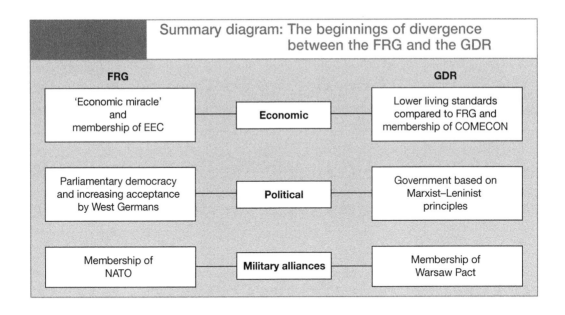

Summary diagram: The beginnings of divergence between the FRG and the GDR

FRG — **GDR**

'Economic miracle' and membership of EEC — **Economic** — Lower living standards compared to FRG and membership of COMECON

Parliamentary democracy and increasing acceptance by West Germans — **Political** — Government based on Marxist–Leninist principles

Membership of NATO — **Military alliances** — Membership of Warsaw Pact

2 | Developments in the FRG Under Adenauer

The 'economic miracle' and rising living standards in the FRG

Key question
What led to West Germany's 'economic miracle' in the 1950s?

During the 1950s the FRG experienced significant economic growth. This was first described by Western observers as an 'economic miracle', which in many ways is an entirely appropriate description. Within a decade, the FRG emerged from devastation and ashes and had built modern towns and cities. It had such a thriving economy that it became desperately short of labour. By the 1960s, the FRG had become one of the most successful

Western economies. In little more than 10 years the FRG had developed into the world's third strongest industrial state and second in world trade after the USA.

What influence did the Marshall Plan have on the FRG's 'economic miracle'?

Since the end of the Second World War many politicians in the USA had been convinced that significant economic support was needed to create a prosperous, integrated Western Europe which would then be able to contain the spread of socialism. By 1948, the generous economic package labelled the Marshall Plan had been announced (see page 23), and 16 Western European nations had benefited from the arrangements, which included a commitment to supporting the FRG's economic development. According to Susan Stern there is still today a widespread myth among many Germans that they were the sole beneficiaries of Marshall Aid and that it was almost entirely the reason for West Germany's rapid post-war economic recovery. In fact, the FRG received significantly smaller amounts of Marshall Aid compared to the other major Western European powers, as shown in Table 2.6.

Table 2.6: Amount received by major Western Europe powers with Marshall Aid (in US dollars)

UK	3.2 billion
France	2.7 billion
FRG	1.4 billion

Marshall Aid significantly supported the development of the FRG in other ways. The USA's commitment of Marshall Aid to the FRG helped to deliver a sense of confidence for investment. It also strengthened Adenauer's political position and helped to create a feeling of national stability that encouraged economic growth. However, Marshall Aid was only one of many factors which contributed to the FRG's 'economic miracle'.

Key date

Start of the Korean War: 1950

Other factors contributing to the economic growth

- The 1948 currency reform had successfully stemmed rising inflation. The **Bundesbank** maintained its policies to control **inflation** and this contributed to confidence in the FRG's economy. The currency reform had also stopped the relatively high rate of absenteeism from work as people now wanted to earn the new currency.
- In spite of the bombing raids, Germany had a sound base on which to build. Much of the industrial infrastructure emerged unscathed. Where wartime damage had to be repaired it prompted the construction of new factories with modern methods of production.
- The FRG had an ample supply of raw materials; notably in the Ruhr area.
- There was also a constant flow of available labour, initially from the GDR, and later from southern Europe and Turkey. The **guest workers**, on fixed-term contracts and without rights of permanent residence, tended to be cheap to employ. This was because they made fewer demands on welfare costs. They were young, healthy and came initially without dependants.
- The Korean War in 1950 was an extremely important factor in stimulating demand for steel in the manufacture of equipment needed for the US war effort. The output of the FRG's

Key terms

Bundesbank
The FRG's central bank.

Inflation
A process in which money declines in value and prices rise as a consequence.

Guest workers
The name given to workers who came to the FRG from Turkey and other parts of southern Europe.

Guest workers in their living accommodation in Frankfurt in 1959.

mechanical engineering almost doubled industry between 1950 and 1952.

- Before 1955 the FRG did not have to finance armed forces or armaments.
- Industrial relations were generally very good. The principle of **co-determination**, established first in the British zone, gave trade union representation on the boards of companies. This involvement gave trade unions a stake in industries and reduced industrial disputes and working time.
- It was also undoubtedly down to the sheer hard work of many Germans themselves. This is obviously difficult to quantify but the willingness of many to work long hours should not be underestimated.
- The policies of the CDU Economics Minister Ludwig Erhard, nicknamed 'Mr Economic Miracle'.

Key term

Co-determination
The principle that workers would be represented at management levels in industry to help develop and maintain sound industrial relations by co-operation and negotiation.

Key question
What were the key features of Erhard's social-market economy?

The social-market economy

Erhard, Adenauer's Minister of Economics, followed the principles of a social-market economy, which allowed free markets to operate while at the same time workers' rights were strengthened. State intervention in the economy was also limited, although the government did regulate certain areas, such as primary industries producing raw materials and food, public transport and housing. The effects of Allied bombing meant that rebuilding many of the FRG's shattered towns and cities was a priority and a specific Ministry of Housing was set up to organise this. Among the programmes adopted were public-housing schemes and the provision of tax incentives for private building companies to construct housing. This helped to provide desperately needed accommodation and also provided employment, thereby contributing to economic growth. By the 1950s Erhard could claim there was full employment in the FRG, which meant that those emigrating from the GDR could easily find employment.

Industrial relations

The FRG also developed successful and highly regarded industrial relations. The principle of co-determination was applied throughout the FRG with the co-determination law of 1951 which gave workers representation at managerial level in large coal and steel companies. Further legislation the following year set up workers' councils in smaller organisations. This encouraged cordial and consensual relations that came to be envied by many other Western states. There was an impressive strike-free record, and a strong sense of responsibility from trade unions towards rebuilding the FRG. The increasing prosperity allowed agreements with trade unions such as the implementation of a five-day week which the unions had campaigned for with a poster of a child and the slogan 'On Saturday, daddy belongs to me'.

Overall prosperity

From the early 1950s onwards there was a clear trend of rising living standards. The FRG's growing economic strength allowed the government to provide effective social welfare provision, although the generous levels of welfare payments were later to cause problems for West German governments in the 1980s. In 1952, tax levies on the rich in the Equalisation of Burdens Law financed the settlement of nearly 10 million refugees from the former German territories in the east and funded an increase in old-age pensions in 1957. Since pensions were now linked to wage increases, pensioners also benefited from the economic miracle.

West Germany's steps to independence

The strength of the economy also smoothed the path to the FRG's independence in 1955. When the FRG was created in 1949 it had no power to pursue an independent foreign policy, and the **Allied High Commission** retained a great deal of control. Adenauer's policies secured independence within six years. Through a policy of economic co-operation with the West, he was able to reduce the fears from other Western European states (notably France) of a resurgent, militaristic Germany, and the strength of the FRG's economy made it an attractive partner. In 1949 Adenauer agreed to support international control of the industrial Ruhr area and this decision eventually led to the FRG being able to form diplomatic relations with other states. Together with France, Belgium, The Netherlands and Luxembourg, the FRG signed the Treaty of Paris in 1951 which created the European Coal and Steel Community (ECSC).

Adenauer's acceptance of international control of the Ruhr was bitterly opposed in the *Bundestag*, but was a significant step towards his goal of the FRG's acceptance within Europe. In fact, the much-resented International Ruhr Authority was short-lived. Its role was ended with the creation of the ECSC, which later led to the formation of the EEC, the forerunner to today's European Union (EU). In 1954 the Allied High Commission was also abolished and the FRG was accepted as an independent state by the Paris–Bonn Treaties which came into force the following year.

> **Key term**
>
> **Allied High Commission**
> Set up under the Basic Treaty, it retained ultimate authority over the constitution and the legislation of the FRG.

> **Key dates**
>
> Signing of the European Coal and Steel (ECSC) Treaty in Paris: 1951
>
> The FRG is recognised as an independent state: 1955

Key question
Why was Adenauer in
power for so long?

Adenauer in power

When Adenauer became Chancellor it was intended by the
CDU/CSU that he would be their leader for only a few years. In
the event, Adenauer remained as Chancellor of the FRG for
14 years, a longer period than either the Weimar Republic or the
Third Reich. In 1957 the CDU/CSU was the first political party
ever to gain an overall majority in German history.

Why was Adenauer able to stay in power for so long?

• The rapid economic development was a key factor in keeping
  the CDU and Adenauer in power. The 'economic miracle'
  created stability which contributed towards the successful
  development of democracy in post-war FRG.
• Other Cold War threats to the FRG, either supposed or real,
  contributed to Adenauer's popularity. Adenauer gained support
  when he successfully secured the release of remaining German
  prisoners of war from the USSR in 1955, in return for West
  German diplomatic recognition of the USSR. The Hungarian

Profile: Konrad Adenauer 1876–1967

1876	– Born in Cologne
1917–33	– Mayor of Cologne
1944	– Imprisoned as an opponent of the Nazis after the **July Bomb Plot**
1949–63	– CDU Chancellor of the FRG winning four successive federal elections

Key term

July Bomb Plot
The attempted
assassination of
Hitler by
German army
officers in 1944.

Adenauer is highly regarded by many as the 'father of modern
Germany'. On the one hand, he is credited with the achievements
of the economic miracle, integrating the FRG successfully with
the West, transforming the FRG into a successfully functioning
democracy and managing the steps to its independence in the years
1949–55. He was voted greatest German in a German opinion
poll in 2002. His opposition to the prospect of a neutral united
Germany and his pursuit of remilitarisation were instrumental in
securing West Germany's membership of NATO and its role as a
sovereign state. However, this policy of strength towards the
USSR perpetuated Germany's division. It tied the FRG to the
Western Allies, and abandoned the GDR's future to the USSR.

Opponents referred to him as the 'Allies' Chancellor' and
perceived him as being too dependent on the West. It is also
worth noting that his own published diaries do not include the
actual period when the Berlin Wall was built. His authoritarian
control of his own government ministers led to criticisms that he
was running a 'Chancellor democracy'. It can also be argued that
most of the more difficult decisions had already been taken by the
Allies during their initial post-war occupation of Germany.

However, the foresight and strength of purpose he showed in
relation to the Ruhr issue in 1949 can be seen as the key to the
achievement of the FRG's independence.

Revolt of 1956 produced fears of a mounting instability in Eastern Europe and so contributed to increased support for the CDU/CSU in the FRG.

- Adenauer's CDU government also benefited from a lack of effective opposition from the SPD. With so much support for Adenauer, the SPD found itself in a political wilderness. Its left-wing politics made it easy for the CDU to link it unfavourably with the GDR. In many ways, Adenauer was the right sort of personality for immediate post-war Germany. His 'father-like' persona, as well as his hierarchical and authoritative stance, was well suited to the times.

Criticisms of the CDU/CSU governments of the FRG in the 1950s

Key question
Why did opposition grow in the 1950s?

These social and economic trends provided a firm political foundation for the FRG, but they were later increasingly criticised by the younger generation. Some highly acclaimed West German authors also commented unfavourably on them. Heinrich Böll's *The Bread of Those Early Years* and Günter Grass's *The Tin Drum* are two examples. Opponents argued that West Germans were becoming too preoccupied with materialism and consumerism and were failing to confront their recent past. Some argued that Erhard's economic policies (and his cigar-smoking image) were more about the creation of wealth rather than the creation of social equality, and that the economic miracle was fuelled by refugees and guest workers on very low wages. There were growing tensions with a new, younger generation that was starting to challenge and question their parents about the extent of their participation in the Third Reich.

Key dates
West German Communist Party (KPD) was declared unconstitutional in the FRG: 1956

Adenauer resigned and was succeeded by Erhard: 1963

The 1951 '131 law' allowed former Nazis to be employed in the civil service, and is sometimes referred to as 'conservative restoration'. Adenauer justified the law on the grounds that the government and civil service desperately needed people with experience. The law was extended to over 150,000 individuals who had previously lost their jobs under denazification. This was popular with the right-wing but created widespread criticism from the left, especially about certain members in Adenauer's government. One controversial appointment was Hans Globke, who was in Adenauer's cabinet from 1953 to 1963. He had played a key role in writing the Nazi **Nuremberg Laws** of 1935. Adenauer's Minister for Refugees, Hans Krüger, had participated in Hitler's **Beer Hall** *Putsch* in 1923. He was eventually dismissed from Adenauer's government when it was revealed that he had been involved in Nazi war crimes, although the charges against him were eventually dropped because of insufficient evidence.

Key terms
Nuremberg Laws A series of anti-Jewish laws passed in Nazi Germany in 1935; included the prohibition of sexual relations and marriage between Jews and Aryans.

Beer Hall *Putsch* Hitler's failed attempt in Munich in November 1923 to overthrow the Bavarian government.

There were also concerns that the guest workers from southern Europe were treated as a social underclass and that this challenged the FRG's bold claims about being a healthy democracy. The guest workers comprised some eight million workers who came to the FRG mainly from Italy, Yugoslavia and Turkey and took up much of the low-paid and unskilled employment. The West German government intended that they

Profile: Ludwig Erhard 1897–1977

1897	– Born in Fürth, southern Germany
1916–18	– Served and was wounded in the First World War
1919–25	– Studied economics
1925–8	– Executive in his parents' business
1928–42	– Worked in, and eventually headed an economic research institute
1942	– Removed from his position by the Nazis for writings contrary to Nazi policy
1945–8	– Economic consultant to the Western Allies
1948	– Director of Economic Council of Bizonia
1948	– Architect of currency reform
1949–63	– Minster of Economics
1963–6	– Chancellor of FRG
1966–77	– Continued as an MP until he died

Due to injuries he had suffered as a soldier in the First World War, Erhard was not conscripted during the Second World War. During the Second World War he wrote a study on the economic problems of the war, which he believed Germany was going to lose. In the immediate post-war period he worked with the USA as an economic consultant for their zone of occupation. He then masterminded the economic policies for Bizonia and currency reform (see page 24).

Erhard became the FRG's first Economics Minister in Adenauer's governments from 1949 to 1963. He is credited with the development of the social-market economy (see page 43) and he presided over the FRG's 'economic miracle'. The economic success of this period contributed significantly to the FRG's subsequent political stability.

Following Adenauer's resignation, Erhard served as Chancellor from 1963 to 1966. Initially his government was popular and he secured an impressive election victory in September 1965, when the CDU/CSU won 48 per cent of the vote. He proved to be less politically adept than he had been economically, and his period in office as Chancellor was short lived. Unfavourable circumstances also contributed to his unexpected lack of success as Chancellor. By the mid-1960s there were concerns over inflation and the extent of government spending, which Erhard attempted to address after the election. The attempts to check inflation bought about over-correction and an economic slowdown, with associated unemployment and hardship. This dented confidence in Erhard's image of economic competence and lost his party electoral support. His attempts to balance the government budget by raising taxes led to splits in the governing coalition and the resignation of FDP cabinet ministers in November 1966. Without a ruling majority in the federal parliament, Erhard resigned and was replaced by Kurt Kiesinger who became Chancellor of the CDU/CSU-SPD 'Grand Coalition'.

would stay in Germany only temporarily and then return home. However, many were later joined by their families and settled in the FRG permanently. By the 1970s they made up about 10 per cent of the West German workforce.

Some left-wing commentators also felt that the FRG was moving in a very narrow 'conservative' direction towards fascism. The West German Communist Party (KPD) was banned in FRG in 1956 for its support of the crushing of the June 1953 uprising in the GDR. Adenauer was undeniably conservative in outlook – one of his major slogans in the 1950s was 'No experiments'. In 1962 Adenauer's reputation was severely damaged by what became known as the *Spiegel* **affair** and he resigned in 1963 at the age of 87 to be succeeded as Chancellor by his Economics Minister, Erhard. The government's actions in the *Spiegel* affair demonstrated Adenauer's authoritarian manner and led to criticisms about the lack of freedom of the press.

The *Spiegel* affair: 1962

Key date

Spiegel **affair**
A scandal following the revelation that journalists working for *Spiegel* magazine were arrested after criticising the FRG's armed forces.

Key term

Remilitarisation of the FRG and membership of NATO

Following rearmament in the mid-1950s both Germanys had armed forces facing each other across a heavily guarded and an increasingly sophisticated 'inner-German' border which represented the frontline of the Cold War for the next 28 years. The integration of the FRG into NATO and the GDR into the Warsaw Pact were seen by opponents in both Germanys as a 'balance of terror' on German soil.

Key question
What issues were involved in the remilitarisation of the FRG?

The remilitarisation of both Germanys was extremely controversial, both at home and abroad. In the FRG there was fierce opposition, especially from Schumacher's SPD, from those with anti-militarist or neutralist feelings, and from those who felt it would severely reduce the possibility of German reunification. Many women who had recently lost their husbands now resented their sons being recruited to the armed forces. There were those in other countries who feared a resurgent, powerful Germany, and there were still unresolved questions over Germany's borders. It was really only the USA that argued that the FRG needed to be a significant part of Western European defence. Although both Germanys remilitarised from the early 1950s onwards, it was not until after reunification that both Germany and the wider international community felt at ease with the deployment of German armed forces abroad. Both the GDR and the FRG had to come to terms with the fact that in the 1950s they were now firm allies of former enemies.

Adenauer argued that the FRG needed to remilitarise. He claimed that the 10,000 German soldiers still being held in Soviet prisoner of war camps, and the USSR's actions such as the Berlin Blockade showed that from the USSR's perspective, the Second World War had not ended. He felt that the FRG would be powerless if the USSR decided to attack the West, and that the FRG's borders were the very frontline of the Cold War. Adenauer also maintained that rearmament, rather than reducing the likelihood of German reunification, would actually make it more probable and that reunification could take place when the West was strong enough to prevent Soviet expansion. Schumacher opposed this, asserting that the West was using Germany for its own purposes. The SPD was keen to introduce nationalist elements in their political programme as it was felt the lack of these had been a major reason for its loss of support to the Nazis in the final years of the Weimar Republic. But, again the international context played a determining role.

The USA had first suggested the FRG became part of NATO in 1950. At the time, Cold War tensions were especially taut because of the conflict in Korea. Clearly, the USA saw the FRG as the frontline of the Cold War in Europe. This was a sharp U-turn in Allied policy. At Potsdam, indefinite German disarmament had been agreed and now suddenly the FRG was seen to be at the very forefront of European and wider international security. There were however, deep divisions in the CDU about whether the FRG's interests were best served by integration with Western Europe and the USA; but it was a policy strongly advocated by Adenauer.

The impact of remilitarisation in the FRG

Eventually in 1955 the FRG joined NATO. This move was controversial within the FRG. The NATO alliance included the USA's nuclear capability, and many Germans were deeply worried that such destructive weapons would be deployed on their own soil and could feasibly be used against the 'other Germany'. West Berlin continued to occupy a unique position. It continued to be under Western Allied occupation and throughout its existence the FRG was never permitted to station any of its own armed forces there. A general system of compulsory military service for 15 months was introduced and considered necessary if Germany was to contribute effectively to NATO's forces. This met widespread opposition from the West German public, which included an effective 'without me' campaign. Some West Germans avoided compulsory military service by moving to West Berlin. Later, a civilian service alternative to national military service was introduced which included work in areas such as hospitals or retirement homes. Although this service was for a longer period, it became so popular that there were discussions in the late 1980s about the possibility of extending compulsory military service to women.

Key term

Bundeswehr
The FRG's armed forces were set up in 1955 with initially only a defensive role.

The setting up of the West German army also meant an amendment to the Basic Law of 1949 (see page 27). A clause was inserted which stated that the FRG's army could be used only for defence and not for offensive action. A year later in January 1956, Adenauer made his first visit to the *Bundeswehr*. In 1957 the Iron Cross Medal (with the swastika removed) was reintroduced into the West German army. By 1961 the FRG was the second strongest force in NATO with 350,000 soldiers. This figure rose to half a million in the 1970s. There were some criticisms that West German army officers were appointed who had previously served during the Third Reich. Adenauer responded curtly to this by declaring that he could not expect NATO to accept the appointment of 18 year olds as army officers.

There was, however, still a degree of hesitancy and caution about West German troops being deployed internationally. In 1965, the FRG government felt unable to respond to US President Johnson's request for 1000 FRG troops to be used in Vietnam.

The end of the 'economic miracle'?

By the mid-1960s, there were signs that the 'economic miracle' had run its course. The FRG entered a mini-recession, with increasing unemployment and rising inflation. West German exports were facing stiffer competition. The recession of the 1960s saw the appearance of a far-right political party, the **NPD**, which had some limited success in winning seven seats in some state elections. A major part of its campaign was the exploitation of fears about the number of guest workers in the FRG. There was discussion of banning the NPD in case they won any seats in a federal election, and its members were barred by the East German government from entering the GDR. The reactions and fears created by this mini-recession indicated that the FRG's successful embracing of democracy depended on a successful economy. Some began to argue that it showed that the FRG's democracy was actually fragile and could easily be challenged. These fears and comments brought back memories of the economic recession that had destroyed the Weimar Republic and had prepared the way for Hitler's rise to power.

NPD
National German Party: a right-wing political party formed in 1964, which gained some seats in state elections in the later 1960s.

Key term

The end of the CDU/CSU government in the FRG

The end of CDU/CSU dominance was partly due to the SPD's changed policies. In 1959, the SPD reformed itself with the Bad Godesberg programme which aimed at widening its electoral appeal. The SPD's traditional support came from the working class, which was now a diminishing proportion of the electorate following the FRG's rapid economic progress. The SPD discarded much of its left-wing rhetoric and rather than portraying itself as a working-class political party it now rebranded itself as a 'people's party'. The SPD changed its policies to support private enterprise, the FRG's membership of NATO and rearmament.

Key question
What factors explain the end of the CDU's dominance of federal politics?

The mini-recession brought an end to Erhard's government in 1966 and led to the 'Grand Coalition' formed with the CDU/CSU and the SPD, with Kiesinger as Chancellor and Brandt as Foreign Minister. Brandt had been Mayor of West Berlin from 1957 to 1966, an experience that clearly had an impact on his beliefs and policies (see pages 79–80). Brandt's attitude and anger over Berlin and his views on Eastern Europe were soon to bring him much support. However, unfortunately for the Grand Coalition, Kiesinger was a former member of the Nazi Party. This led to increased domestic opposition and the emergence of a radical student movement.

Formation of the 'Grand Coalition' between the CDU/CSU and the SPD: 1966

Key date

The reasons for the ending of this period of the CDU's dominance of politics should also be set in the wider context of political and social changes within the FRG. Eichmann's trial in Jerusalem and the second series of Auschwitz trials in Frankfurt were also calling widespread attention to Germany's recent past, both at home and abroad. Many in the FRG felt these issues had been ignored by Adenauer's governments. Furthermore, there was widespread concern in the FRG about the USA's involvement in Vietnam. Inside the FRG, many were still frustrated by the lack of any progress regarding the Berlin question and relations between the two Germanys. The continued division of Germany and general attitudes towards it were characterised for many by the 1968 Olympic Games, which saw an 'East Germany' team representing the GDR and a 'Germany' team representing the FRG.

Summary diagram: Developments in the FRG under Adenauer		
Strengths	**Politics** • Sucessfully functioning democracy • Integration with Western Europe and USA • Political stability • Independence	**Economy** • Social-market economy • Economic miracle • Rising living standards • Overall prosperity • Good industrial relations • Major world economic power
Weaknesses	• Criticisms of 131 law • *Spiegel* affair • Growth of criticism from both left-wing and right-wing groups	• Treatment of guest workers • Mini-recession mid-1960s

3 | Developments in the GDR Under Ulbricht 1950–71

Political control by the SED

Key question
How did the SED control the GDR?

Under Ulbricht's leadership the SED began to transform the GDR radically. The period 1949–61 was officially labelled 'the creation of the basis of socialism'. In Marxist–Leninist theory the socialist party (in this case the SED) had the role of guiding society through this transitional phase, during which the old, established capitalist order would be removed and the masses would be awoken from their 'false consciousness'. This was the Marxist–Leninist theoretical basis for the SED's control of the other political parties and the mass organisations. This was their rationale for the electoral system in the GDR. Elections were not genuine expressions of democratic choice; voters were simply presented with a list of government-nominated candidates. The number of seats in the *Volkskammer* was predetermined and it was considered democratic to maintain the SED's leading role because it provided guidance to the electorate. It saw itself as having a clear and essential role in transmitting socialist beliefs to the masses. In spite of the SED's electoral dominance, recent research by Jeannette Madarasz suggested that the amount of success that the SED actually had in winning over the hearts and minds of the GDR population in the 1950s was limited.

State control of agriculture and industry

The GDR pursued policies of state ownership of agriculture and industry, which were modelled on the policies pursued by Stalin in the USSR in the 1930s. In July 1952, at the second party conference, the SED announced that it would be taking more industry and agriculture into state ownership. It also stressed that economic priorities would be with heavy industry (which implied it would be at the expense of consumer goods) and that the five historic *Länder* would be replaced with 15 new administrative districts (*Bezirke*) controlled centrally from East Berlin. By the late 1950s, all energy production and major industries were in the hands of the state and many farms had been **collectivised**. The GDR reached the end of its first five-year economic plan in 1955 and in spite of the serious difficulties and challenges it faced, it did succeed in doubling its industrial production. However, the scarcity of consumer goods and the failure to raise living standards did little to encourage public support for the government. Many East Germans continued to make unfavourable comparisons between their own living standards and those in the FRG.

The impact of collectivisation

Collectivisation was followed in order to increase the size of farms and to exploit both machinery and agricultural labour to the full. In spite of the human costs this was ultimately successful and productivity increased (see page 66).

Although the SED portrayed collectivisation as a progressive revolutionary process, many farmers rejected it as the destruction of their traditional ways of living and working. At this particular point in the early 1950s, farmers were one of the groups that were leaving the GDR for the West in disproportionately high numbers. Up to 15,000 East German farmers left during the 1950s for the FRG rather than be forced into collectivisation. Later, in the 1950s, a second period of collectivisation led to further food shortages. Enforced collectivisation was carried out in such a way that East German bishops protested to the GDR government about what they saw as a disregard for human rights. Collectivisation, combined with the emigration of skilled farmers, contributed to the heavy rationing, which included many basic items such as milk and butter. Rationing did not end in the GDR until 1958. The rate of collectivisation is shown in Table 2.7.

Lack of overall popular support for the GDR

Overall morale in the general population was low. Turnout for the May Day parades was often thin, despite SED efforts to encourage attendance. There was also a desperate shortage of housing, and resentment from small businesses. The SED continued to increase its control and influence over most areas of people's lives and there was a general culture of repression. Some Christian organisations were declared illegal. It was increasingly difficult for people to leave for the FRG, and teachers and pupils were indoctrinated in Marxism–Leninism. The USSR urged the SED to try to reduce tension by easing travel between the two Germanys,

Key question
How did agriculture and industry develop?

Key term

Collectivisation
Private farms being taken over by state co-operatives.

Table 2.7:
Percentage of agricultural land collectivised in the GDR 1951–71

1951	3
1953	12
1955	20
1957	25
1959	37
1961	84
1963	85
1965	85
1967	86
1969	86
1971	86

Key question
What support was there for the GDR government by the general population?

and to allow some private industries to have state loans. The USSR believed this would reduce some of the discontent, as well as leave the way more open for the possible reunification of East and West Germany. However, Ulbricht refused to adopt these measures. Furthermore, his announcement that there needed to be a 10 per cent increase in industrial productivity led to widespread resentment from many workers. In the climate of general discontent, it was this central government directive that triggered the events which have become known as the June uprising.

The June 1953 uprising

On 16 June 1953 East German builders working on the new prestigious and propaganda showpiece **Stalinallee** in east-central Berlin downed their tools in protest at the demanded increase in work norms which was not being met with a rise in the standard of living. This began a strike which soon spread across the entire GDR. Workers marched to the government offices, which at that time were in one of the very few governmental buildings in central Berlin which had not been destroyed during the Second World War. They were spontaneously joined by thousands of other workers, and began demanding free elections, a general strike, and the resignation of the government. Their chants included 'We don't want a national army, we want butter'. Some of the strikers tore down the USSR's flag on top of the historic

Key question
Why was there an uprising in 1953?

Key date

June uprising in the GDR: 1953

Key term

Stalinallee
A major street in East Berlin, later named Karl-Marx Allee as part of de-Stalinisation in 1961. Its spacious apartments remained desirable throughout the history of the GDR.

East German workers throwing stones at Soviet tanks in East Berlin during the June 1953 uprising.

Brandenburg Gate and then ceremoniously set it on fire. The news soon spread, and by the next day similar protests and strikes of up to half a million workers were reported in over 200 cities and towns throughout the GDR.

The anger became increasingly directed towards the USSR, rather than towards the government of the GDR or Ulbricht himself. Eventually the Soviet army had to intervene with 600 tanks and 20,000 soldiers: the first time Soviet forces were used in an Eastern bloc state to crush a rebellion. The Soviet forces were used to hold strategic positions such as the docks on the GDR's Baltic coast, major railway stations and the borders with West Berlin. Officially, there were 21 deaths, but some estimate it was nearer 50. Afterwards at least 20 people were executed and 6000 arrested of whom 500 received life sentences. The GDR authorities and SED-controlled newspapers claimed that the uprising had been initiated by the FRG's interference in the GDR's own affairs, and that it was part of the USA's wider plans to overthrow the GDR. Traditionally the uprising has been portrayed as a revolt by industrial workers in Berlin and other major towns or cities in the GDR. However, relatively recent work argues that there was also support and widespread discontent in rural areas.

What was the impact of the 1953 uprising?

Death of Stalin: 1953   **Key date**

- In the long term it served to consolidate authoritarian rule in the GDR. Ulbricht was concerned that his own position had been made vulnerable by the scale of the revolt and his reliance on assistance from the USSR to crush it. He was also worried that he might be weakened by the change of leaders in the USSR following Stalin's death in March 1953. His successor Khrushchev followed a policy of de-Stalinisation and Ulbricht was known to have been closely associated with Stalin. However, the events strengthened Ulbricht's position. He was able to use the 1953 uprising as an opportunity to justify a purge of the SED of any remaining SPD members. Ulbricht's reputation with the USSR actually rose in 1956 when a wave of rebellions in the Eastern bloc, culminating in the Hungarian uprising did not spread to the GDR.
- The USSR now felt obliged to declare its formal recognition of the GDR. Following the 1953 uprising, the USSR further increased its influence in the Eastern bloc with COMECON. This was an organisation structured on very similar lines to the EEC in Western Europe, which aimed at developing trade within the Eastern bloc.
- Events had also shown the GDR and the USSR that the Western powers had not been willing to intervene outside their own zones.
- The 1953 June uprising also had a far-reaching political impact in the FRG. The West German Communist Party had supported the suppression of the rising. This led to Adenauer banning West Germany's KPD, barring its members from state employment and putting many on trial. Some West German communists at this point left the FRG for the GDR. The FRG also made 17 June a day to be commemorated every year in

Profile: Walter Ulbricht 1893–1973

1893	– Born in Leipzig, the son of a tailor
1915–17	– Served on the Eastern Front during the First World War
1920	– Became a member of the German Communist Party
1933–7	– In exile in Paris
1937–45	– In exile in the USSR
1945	– Led the 'Ulbricht' group in Berlin to set up a KPD along Stalinist lines
1950	– General Secretary of the SED
1960	– Head of State for the GDR
1971	– Forced to resign

Ulbricht was the leader of a group of Soviet-trained German socialist exiles who arrived in Berlin at the end of the Second World War. During his time in exile he had translated and interrogated captured German officers, had prepared anti-Nazi propaganda broadcasts for the USSR, and had addressed a communist rally to German soldiers captured by the USSR as prisoners of war following the **Battle of Stalingrad**.

As General Secretary of the SED his own position seemed vulnerable during the June 1953 uprising, but subsequently the uprising served to consolidate his rule in the GDR and he became Head of State in 1960. He was also responsible for the decision to construct the Berlin Wall in 1961. His government increased the rate of collectivisation, but also introduced the 'New Economic System' in July 1963. Ulbricht's reduction of central controls in the NES had some initial success in increasing production, but further liberalisation was vetoed and the NES was abandoned when Honecker's influence grew at the end of the 1960s. We cannot know what success Ulbricht's plans would have brought. However, the return to an emphasis on centralised planning and control partially accounts for the accumulation of economic problems in the GDR by the end of the 1980s.

Ulbricht's proud proclamations that the GDR was a model of modern, successful socialism created tension with the USSR, which resented his implied superiority of the GDR to the USSR. Changing international relations, with the emergence of *détente* in the late 1960s and moves towards a new GDR–FRG relationship with Brandt's *Ostpolitik* (see Chapter 3), further worried the USSR.

Traditionally, Ulbricht's downfall has been primarily explained by his stance as an ardent Stalinist which led him to resist the FRG's *Ostpolitik*. However, some recent views suggest that his downfall was a combination of internal conspiracy in the SED, and the fears of the USSR. The USSR was concerned that Ulbricht might begin making separate agreements with the FRG and break away from the official line dictated by the USSR to its Warsaw Pact members.

Ulbricht resigned in 1971 and was replaced by Honecker. In 1973 he died and received a very low-profile state funeral.

Key terms

Battle of Stalingrad
A major Soviet victory, 1942–3, over Germany during the Second World War, which marked a downturn in Germany's military fortunes.

Détente
The reduction in tension between the USA and the USSR from the late 1960s to the early 1980s.

the FRG as a day of national unity. This was misleading as the demonstration by the GDR workers had not been about German reunification. Other national days had different interpretations in both Germanys. The GDR celebrated 8 May 1945 as the anniversary of the overthrowing of the Third Reich by the USSR and the liberation of Germany from Nazism. The same day in the FRG was often a day of grief and reflection for the human losses incurred during the Second World War.

The Ministry for State Security (*Stasi*)

In 1950, the GDR parliament passed a law to set up a Ministry for State Security (*Staatssicherheit*, abbreviated to **Stasi**) – 'the Sword and Shield of the Party' – with its clear and direct links to the SED. Its main function was to use surveillance to prevent disturbances by exposing pockets of opposition. It also had powers to find and arrest opponents of the GDR government. Most of its leaders were long-serving communists and it had up to 15,000 full-time employees by the mid-1950s. In some respects, 'the firm' (as it was known in colloquial German) failed in its main role to discover signs of dissent; as shown by its inability to prevent the June 1953 uprising, a failure which led to Ulbricht's

Key question
How was the *Stasi* organised?

Stasi
GDR's Ministry for State Security, set up in 1950, which developed extensive surveillance both within the GDR and internationally.

Key term

Profile: Erich Mielke 1907–2000

1907	– Born in Berlin
1924	– Joined the German Communist Party
1931	– Murdered two police officers
1932	– Attended the Comintern school
1936–9	– Fought in the Spanish Civil War
1957–89	– Head of the *Stasi*
1993	– Sentenced to six years' imprisonment for the murders in 1931 but paroled in 1995
2000	– Died in Berlin

Mielke became a member of the German Communist Party (KPD) during the 1920s and left Germany for the USSR after murdering two police officers. In the USSR he attended the Lenin School. He returned to Germany in 1945 to support the setting up of security forces. He headed the *Stasi* from 1957 until the collapse of the GDR. He was also known to manipulate the football results of his favourite team, Berliner FC Dynamo, to ensure its position in the first division, which was criticised by his colleagues in the Politburo. Shortly after the opening of the Berlin Wall he was greeted with mass derision during a televised statement when he proclaimed to the East German public 'I love you all'. After the reuniting of Germany in October 1990, he was arrested and sentenced to six years' imprisonment for the 1931 murder of the police officers. He was granted parole after less than two years on the grounds of poor health. His unmarked grave is just outside the Friedrichsfelde Cemetery set up in East Berlin in 1951 for communist heroes (which includes the graves of Karl Liebknecht, Rosa Luxemburg and Walter Ulbricht).

swift removal of the *Stasi* Chief Minister, Zaisser. It did, however, play a major role in carrying out arrests in June 1953. Mielke became head of the *Stasi* shortly afterwards and remained its head until the collapse of the GDR in 1989.

Another function of the *Stasi* was to undertake 'mood reports' of the general population. This was also a role that the mass organisations and political parties performed. These reports aimed to collect details of public opinion, and were especially used at critical points in East Germany's history, such as the building of the Berlin Wall and the uprising in Czechoslovakia. They were then used to help inform government policies as well as indicate to the SED where to target their propaganda campaigns. The collection of public opinion suggests that, to some extent, the general public could express their personal opinions.

The role of the IMs

After the uprising in June 1953, the *Stasi* began to recruit **IMs** ('unofficial collaborators'). These were civilians rather than full-time *Stasi* employees, who were often recruited on a short-term basis and were expected to report back on specific individuals to an allocated *Stasi* officer. The *Stasi* grew in size and its role changed in emphasis. In 1953, following the uprising, Ulbricht directed the *Stasi* to concentrate the vast majority of the operations on internal issues within the GDR rather than working on gathering intelligence reports on the West. The number of full-time *Stasi* employees reached 50,000 by the late 1960s, with approximately 100,000 IMs. This grew under Honecker to nearly 100,000 *Stasi* employees and an estimated 300,000 IMs by the mid-1980s. *Stasi* employees also worked as bodyguards for members of the Politburo and their families.

After the reunification of Germany, individuals who had worked for the *Stasi* often found themselves ostracised. Some spoke of their various motives for joining. The *Stasi* used sophisticated and often subtle psychological methods. Many of those recruited were often vulnerable, insecure personalities and the *Stasi* offered them a sense of belonging. One particular group the *Stasi* recruited as IMs were prostitutes. They often worked in hotels that were frequented by Westerners.

Those who worked as IMs have given a variety of reasons. For some, it clearly gave a sense of power; some gained materially and had access to consumer goods otherwise difficult or expensive to obtain, such as a telephone or television. For others, it opened up educational, career and travel opportunities. Being an IM could also bring special privileges; for example one parent with a disabled child became an IM in return for her child's admission to a special school. Others who became IMs believed that they were genuinely making a valuable contribution to the development of the GDR and its future.

The *Stasi* was surrounded by a huge sense of secrecy. For example, those awarded a *Stasi* medal could not keep it in case somebody else discovered it. There were also instances where individuals would try to leave but feared the reprisals that might then be taken against them. The *Stasi* did, however, find it hard to recruit IMs from the most disaffected in the GDR, who were the very individuals it most needed in order to infiltrate opposition. In time, the *Stasi* came to be regarded as one of the most successful intelligence agencies in the world. You will find more on the work of the *Stasi* in Chapter 4 and its legacy in a reunited Germany in Chapter 5.

Remilitarisation of the GDR and membership of the Warsaw Pact

In May 1955 the Warsaw Pact was formed as a military alliance of the USSR and its Eastern bloc satellite states. This was in many ways a direct response to the formation of NATO.

In 1955 the NVA (National People's Army) was formed in the GDR (which somewhat oddly kept the Prussian goose-step march throughout its existence, with clear images of the Third Reich). The GDR government stressed to its citizens the need for the GDR to defend itself against the West's imperial and expansionist ambitions. However, very few volunteered to join, and in 1962, after the construction of the Berlin Wall (see page 64), the GDR government introduced compulsory military service. Several factors account for the lack of support for the NVA:

- The GDR's labour shortage made it difficult to find sufficient numbers willing to join the NVA.
- Military spending on the NVA was unpopular when many East Germans felt that money could clearly be much better spent on improving people's living standards.
- There was a widespread anti-militaristic attitude. There were also reports that some young people stayed away from the SED mass youth organisation, the FDJ, because it reminded people of the Hitler Youth.
- Many feared that the formation of the army reduced the likelihood of German reunification. Later in 1961 there was also a widespread reluctance from those in the armed forces to join the 'inner-German border' and Berlin Wall patrols, but to admit to this could have serious repercussions for future careers.

With such widespread reluctance, East German bishops urged the government to provide an alternative to compulsory military service. This, although accepted by the GDR government (unlike other Eastern bloc states), often meant work as '**construction soldiers**'. Those that took this option were treated harshly because they were regarded by the authorities as disloyal to the GDR. These individuals also found that it proved to be detrimental to their later career and educational opportunities, and sometimes they even received prison sentences. Even as late as 1981, a proposal by a group from Dresden to the GDR government for an alternative community service such as working in hospitals, retirement homes and schools (such as existed in the FRG) was completely rejected.

Key question
Why did it prove so difficult to recruit to the NVA?

Compulsory military service began in the GDR: 1962

Key date

Construction soldiers
Men who refused conscription to the GDR's armed forces and instead did hard physical labour on projects such as building roads and housing.

Key term

Table 2.8: Numbers of East German border troops who escaped across the 'inner-German border'

Years	Number
1961–5	1385
1966–70	508
1971–5	145
1976–80	37
1981–5	71
1985–9	73

In spite of the recruitment difficulties, the NVA's efficiency was demonstrated in August 1961 with the overnight construction of the border (see page 67) between the Eastern and Western zones of Berlin and the subsequent construction of the Berlin Wall. No other soldiers from any other Eastern bloc country or the USSR were involved in its construction or later defence. In 1968 East German troops, as part of the Warsaw Pact, joined Soviet forces to help crush the revolt in Prague and to suppress attempts at reform in Czechoslovakia. This demonstrated the GDR's firm alliance with the USSR and the reliability of the NVA.

The loyalty of the NVA to the regime was not total. A significant number of border soldiers chose to escape into West Berlin or into the FRG between the building of the Berlin Wall and the end of Germany's division. Table 2.8 shows the numbers of East German border troops who escaped.

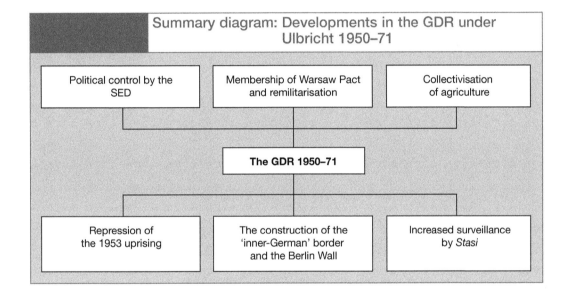

Summary diagram: Developments in the GDR under Ulbricht 1950–71

- Political control by the SED
- Membership of Warsaw Pact and remilitarisation
- Collectivisation of agriculture

The GDR 1950–71

- Repression of the 1953 uprising
- The construction of the 'inner-German' border and the Berlin Wall
- Increased surveillance by *Stasi*

4 | Emigration from the GDR to the FRG and the Building of the Berlin Wall in 1961

Emigration from the GDR in the 1950s

Key question
Why was emigration such a difficult problem for the GDR government?

The 'inner-German border' of more than 1300 km was already heavily fortified by the early 1950s. It was made of high metal fences, and incorporated alarms, trenches and watchtowers; the later Berlin Wall was less than a tenth of this border. In addition to the actual border, on the eastern side there was also a 5-km 'exclusion zone' and a special stamp was required on identity cards to enter this area. Any GDR citizens living in this area who were not regarded as totally loyal to the SED regime were forcibly relocated to areas further inside GDR territory. Border guards were ordered to shoot anybody who did not stop when ordered to at the border. Despite these measures, over three and a half million GDR citizens managed to emigrate from the GDR to the FRG between the setting up of the border and the building of the

Berlin Wall in 1961. In the same period only approximately 50,000 people migrated from West to East Germany. Overall, the population of the GDR fell from 18.5 million in 1950 to just over 17 million in 1961, resulting in an increasingly ageing population in East Germany. In contrast, the FRG rose from a population of 46 million to 56 million during the same period. This obviously created a serious economic problem for the GDR as it became increasingly difficult to manufacture or to farm effectively. Further, and perhaps more importantly, it also made it difficult for the state to develop its own credibility. The continued emigration undermined the GDR's very existence when so many of its own citizens were rejecting it. Table 2.9 shows the numbers of East Germans emigrating to West Berlin and the FRG.

Table 2.9: East Germans emigrating to West Berlin and the FRG

Year	Number of emigrants	Year	Number of emigrants
1949	125,250	1956	279,190
1950	197,780	1957	261,620
1951	165,650	1958	204,060
1952	182,390	1959	143,920
1953	331,390	1960	199,190
1954	184,200	1961	155,400
		(to the building of the Berlin Wall in August)	
1955	252,900		

The crime of 'flight from the republic'

These emigrants were labelled guilty in the GDR of the crime of 'flight from the republic'. Many of those who left were skilled workers that the government desperately needed to keep. It was also politically embarrassing and humiliating to the GDR government. The FRG could use the high numbers migrating west for its own political propaganda about repression and living standards in the GDR which was forcing so many of its citizens to leave. Owing to the economic miracle, the FRG could easily assimilate those leaving the GDR. When GDR citizens arrived in West Berlin they were processed at a reception centre at Marienfeld (and some were even vetted by the West German authorities for work as potential spies). They were able to claim FRG citizenship and, if they could prove they had suffered political persecution (which was relatively easy in the Cold War climate) they received generous financial and housing assistance and were then allocated to various other towns and cities throughout the FRG.

Despite its illegality and the accompanying risk of imprisonment, 'flight from the republic' was still relatively easy in the early to mid-1950s. Individuals could apply for travel visas which were sometimes granted and some simply left the GDR and did not return. But the major problem for the GDR was that it was relatively easy to cross from the eastern sector to the Western sectors in Berlin. The city of Berlin compounded the problem for the GDR authorities because there were also the so-called 50,000 'border-crossers' in or near Berlin, who lived in the GDR but commuted to work daily in the Western zone of Berlin. The GDR discouraged this. Since the 'border-crossers' were paid higher wages in the West, they were perceived by the GDR as being lured towards capitalism and thus represented a dangerous influence on others living in the GDR. Gradually, the GDR reduced the benefits of being a 'border-crosser'. It was made compulsory for them to change a proportion of their wages into East German currency and to pay their bills such as rent and electricity in West German currency, whereas previously for individuals it had always been useful to have disposable Western currency. After the wall was built, many of the former 'border-crossers' were forced to take employment outside Berlin and they were classed as 'politically unreliable'. On maps published in the GDR, West Berlin was simply left unnamed as a blank white space.

The East German government's response to emigration

This situation was clearly a very difficult dilemma for the GDR authorities. They could undertake reforms within the GDR and hope that this would deter the 'flight from the republic' or clamp down and risk mass discontent. From the late 1950s, it became increasingly difficult for GDR citizens to obtain a travel visa; two-thirds of the roads leading from East Berlin into the Western sectors of the city were sealed off, and more key personnel were employed by the *Stasi* in East Berlin to identify those attempting to emigrate. The *Stasi* and East German police looked for suspicious individuals with large amounts of luggage. In addition, mail was often checked by the *Stasi* to see whether individuals were sending treasured possessions west before crossing the border themselves. There was also a major propaganda campaign about how badly former GDR citizens were being treated in the FRG. From 1957, the GDR began imposing sentences of three years in prison on people caught attempting 'flight from the republic'. In the year running up to the building of the Berlin Wall, about 50,000 GDR citizens were arrested for this offence and there was a noticeable increase in early 1961 (see Table 2.9 on page 60) of individuals crossing the border as they sensed that it would be soon their final chance to try and leave.

At this particular stage, those leaving were mainly young, skilled workers that the GDR could ill afford to lose. In an attempt to stem the outflow of trained medical staff, the GDR in 1958 gave doctors certain benefits. They were allowed to practise privately, were able to travel abroad and were given significant advantages to enable their children to gain university places. Nevertheless, the effect of emigration was to threaten the GDR government in a very different way from 1953 – not by an uprising but by a severe haemorrhaging of its population.

A detailed analysis by Patrick Major examined the various fluctuations in the flow of emigration from the GDR to the FRG between 1949 and 1961 and how at various times there were different push and pull factors at work encouraging some individuals to leave the GDR for the FRG (see Table 2.9). During the Cold War, all emigration was interpreted as politically motivated. The FRG could argue that individuals were escaping from the totalitarian GDR regime and the GDR responded by labelling emigrants as deserters from the communist cause. However, Major's analysis showed a more complex picture. In the early post-war period there was still a huge refugee crisis throughout both Germanys and consequently a transient population, with millions still having no sense of 'home' and looking for lost friends and family. Therefore, much of the population movement from east to west may have been due to this refugee crisis, rather than a rejection of the GDR. However, Major's analysis does show that the numbers emigrating from the GDR did tend to increase during periods of increasing internal and international tension, such as after the 1953 uprising and the Hungarian uprising in 1956, as well as in the late 1950s during the second phase of state collectivisation of agriculture.

Comparison of the economies of the FRG and the GDR

Key question
How differently did the economies of the FRG and GDR develop?

The FRG was very successful economically in comparison to its Western European allies. Similarly, the GDR's economy was successful in comparison to its allies in the Eastern bloc. Comparisons of the economies of the two Germanys often highlight the relative scarcity of consumer goods in the GDR, compared with the FRG. These comparisons do not give sufficient weight to the success of the GDR relative to other Eastern bloc states (see pages 107–8). One individual experience exemplifies this. Peter Nikolaev, a Russian who was based in the GDR as a young soldier in October in 1956, still has vivid memories of his first experience of window shopping in the GDR and his sheer amazement at the range of ties on sale – colour and price – compared to the restricted choice to which he was accustomed in the USSR. Nevertheless, there were very marked differences in economic performance of the FRG and the GDR. Table 2.10 suggests some reasons for this.

The Berlin Wall
Reasons for building the Berlin Wall

The East German leadership had serious concerns at extent of migration from the GDR. Despite the risk of harsh penalties and possible imprisonment, many GDR citizens were still being tempted by the FRG's 'economic miracle' and political freedoms. As well as creating severe difficulties for the East German economy, West Berlin was an embarrassing island of capitalism deep inside their territory. Its very existence challenged and undermined the GDR state, and West Berlin was an obvious centre from which Western spies and intelligence operations could operate.

Table 2.10: Reasons for the differences in the economic performance of the FRG and the GDR

FRG's strengths	GDR's weaknesses
The benefits of Marshall Aid.	The USSR's extraction of resources as reparations in the immediate post-war period.
The economic policies followed by Adenauer's governments, including Erhard's social-market economy.	The government's policy of a 'command economy' and its insistence on increasing productivity without an increase in living standards led to widespread discontent.
The availability of cheap labour and the development of harmonious industrial relations.	The continued emigration from the GDR to the FRG of agricultural and industrial workers.
Integration with Western alliances that were committed to ensuring the FRG's economic success as a means to prevent the spread of communism.	Integration with Eastern bloc states whose continued suspicion of a resurgent GDR led to limited economic co-operation.
The success of the EEC enabled the FRG to increase its trade with Western Europe.	COMECON had very limited success in developing trade within the Eastern bloc.

These increasing concerns were also during a period of wider Cold War tensions which grew as a result of events from the late 1950s: the Hungarian rebellion was suppressed by the USSR in 1956, and Castro took power in Cuba in 1959. From the late 1950s onwards the Soviet leader, Khrushchev, had also made a series of announcements claiming that the USSR's nuclear missiles were superior to those of the USA.

Berlin then became the subject of open superpower dispute in 1961. At a meeting in Vienna in the summer between Khrushchev and US President Kennedy, Khrushchev declared that all of Berlin was GDR territory and even threatened outright military action on the issue of the still-divided city. Kennedy's response was a public statement guaranteeing that West Berlin would remain under the control and occupation of the Western Allies.

In the summer of 1961, Ulbricht publicly stated at an international press conference that there was no intention of building a wall. But at the same time he informed the USSR that the continuing migration from the GDR was reaching a crisis point. Following a meeting early in August in 1961 between the leaders of all the Eastern bloc states, Ulbricht was finally given the official go-ahead to proceed with sealing off all routes between the eastern sector and West Berlin. Why was Ulbricht given this support to isolate West Berlin?

Key question
Who was primarily responsible for the building of the wall?

The role of the USSR

The share of responsibility between Ulbricht and Khrushchev for the construction of the Berlin Wall is debated. The main arguments are summarised overleaf.

- Khrushchev had failed to force concessions from the USA regarding the withdrawal of Allied forces from West Berlin and so therefore supported the construction of the Berlin Wall. Khrushchev felt that the mass emigration from the GDR meant that it was becoming an economic liability for the USSR. Therefore action was necessary to deal with the drain of the GDR's population.
- The initiative came from Ulbricht, who put pressure on Khrushchev to take action. Khrushchev felt the need to appease one of the USSR's satellite states. Khrushchev did not want to risk the possibility of nuclear war over Berlin. He was therefore taking a major gamble in his decision to support Ulbricht.

The construction of the wall

Only on the day before construction, 12 August 1961, did Ulbricht finally inform all his own ministers. By 6 a.m. the next morning, the eastern and western sectors were blocked off from each other by barbed wire; and railway lines were cut. Over the next few years, a concrete wall was put up, and the entire border between the two Germanys was strengthened. The construction was done entirely by the GDR army and workers, and did not involve the USSR at all. During its construction, border guards were ordered to shoot any GDR construction workers who attempted to defect. The GDR informed its citizens that it was creating the conditions for peace in Europe and protecting them from the neighbouring fascist state and the imperialist ambitions of the West.

Between 13 August 1961 and 9 November 1989, very few GDR citizens were able to travel West, and West Berliners needed passes to enter East Berlin. Some East Berliners managed to escape quickly through buildings which at that stage were still part of the border. But these were soon demolished. The lack of immediate response from the German population was probably due to the sheer speed of the event, their total surprise and consequent state of shock. It also revealed the extent of repression in the GDR. In fact, no photographs of the border were permitted in the East German press and newspaper articles justified the closing of the border to maintain 'peace-loving socialism'. US President Kennedy, France's President De Gaulle and British Prime Minister Macmillan were all on holiday so it was several days before the Western Allies made a formal protest to the USSR. Adenauer himself did not make a visit to West Berlin until 10 days later – much to the annoyance of Brandt, the Mayor of West Berlin. Although the West made protests through ordinary diplomatic channels, Kennedy made it clear that while the Western Allies could protect West Berliners, any attempt to stand up for the rights of all GDR citizens would probably lead to a huge increase in tension between the superpowers or an embarrassing political climbdown by the West.

> **Key date**
>
> Construction of the Berlin Wall began: 13 August 1961

A woman is lowered from a window in Bernauer Strasse on a rope to escape into the Western sector of Berlin on 10 September 1961, soon after the building of the Berlin Wall.

Key question
What were the effects of the Berlin Wall on West Berlin and the FRG?

The immediate impact of the Berlin Wall on West Berliners and the FRG

Immediately, many families and friends found themselves divided. Those living in West Berlin were concerned about their immediate future now that they were completely encircled by the wall. On the very same day that the border was closed, all telephone lines from West Berlin were cut. There was a demonstration in West Berlin led by their mayor Willy Brandt, who felt that the USA had failed to respond. No one had any idea how the situation might change in the next few days. There were fears in West Berlin about what might come next and removal companies were booked up months ahead as some West Berliners decided to move to the FRG itself. The West's military forces were strengthened in the FRG. In September 1961, the USA sent an additional 40,000 soldiers to Europe, the majority of whom went to the FRG, and the West Germans extended the compulsory military service of 36,000 soldiers by three months who were about to be demobilised and conscription rose from six to 18 months in 1962.

The immediate human impact was to divide families and friends. Although travel visas were later permitted for West Germans to visit East Berlin, the provision was erratic and was at the whim of the GDR authorities. Obtaining a visa also required a payment to the GDR in hard currency. Western currency continued to be attractive to East Berliners too. When visits later resumed, Western visitors' dropping coins in the fountains in East Berlin's central **Alexanderplatz** became a source of Western currency for East Berliners for nearly 30 years. In December 1963, arrangements were made to allow some West Berliners to visit relations over the Christmas and New Year period and further arrangements were developed later. On this first occasion when visits were permitted, Ulbricht ordered strict surveillance of West German visitors by the *Stasi*.

The impact of the Berlin Wall on the GDR

The wall increased stability inside the GDR since many East Germans now simply had to come to terms with life in the GDR. This had the psychological impact of encouraging many to work harder towards creating a successful socialist society.

The SED referred to the division as the 'protective' wall. This propaganda message was repeated throughout the wall's existence despite the fact that many of East Germany's weapons pointed in the direction of its own citizens. In 1986 for example, the GDR issued a set of postage stamps to commemorate the 25th anniversary of the 'anti-fascist protective wall'. Inside the GDR, the wall's very existence made state repression much easier for the government.

The New Economic System

In many ways the construction of the Berlin Wall eased the domestic situation for the GDR government. It stemmed the haemorrhage of labour. It made it far easier for the government confidently to plan domestic and economic policies now that it had a guaranteed labour supply. Soon after the wall was built, many factories had a six-day week introduced. In 1963, Ulbricht proudly announced the 'Age of Socialism and the New Economic System'. This aimed to improve industrial productivity by increasing flexibility. Central state controls were reduced to allow for more decision-making at regional levels, such as factories having more freedom to obtain materials. It also aimed to create more attractive career prospects inside the GDR – especially for those in scientific and technological professions.

By the late 1960s wages had risen, more consumer goods had become available and agricultural production had begun to rise. Although there were still shortages of both housing and food, by the late 1960s Ulbricht was optimistically claiming that the GDR

Key term

Alexanderplatz
A major square in Berlin which became the centre of East Berlin. It witnessed the largest public demonstration in the GDR on 4 November 1989.

would soon be overtaking the FRG economically. However, a changed political climate and the GDR's subservience to Moscow brought an end to the New Economic System in the late 1960s. Following the Prague uprising in Czechoslovakia in 1968, the USSR was unwilling for its satellite states to experiment and so the process of centralisation was renewed.

Key question
How did the Berlin Wall change during its existence?

The development of the Berlin Wall and the 'inner-German border'

The wall became iconic and had propaganda value for the West. It was used constantly to show the repression, not just in the GDR, but in the entire Eastern bloc. The view of the wall from West Berlin was very different from the view of the wall from East Berlin. In the West it was graffiti covered; people could go right up to it and touch it. In places, there was some very impressive artwork; political comments were sprayed along it and there were some expletives. Despite the suffering it caused for many Germans, in West Berlin it became a major tourist attraction with viewing platforms for people to look on 'the other side'. In the east it was whitewashed and there was certainly no graffiti, it was heavily guarded and there was a large exclusion zone. In East Berlin, many buildings near the wall were government offices in a heavily guarded and restricted zone.

Although initially formed of barbed wire, it was later constructed as a concrete wall with further modifications made in 1975 and 1980. It was strengthened constantly and made more sophisticated throughout the existence of the GDR with many

The original barbed wire 'wall' being replaced with concrete. This photograph shows work being done on a section of the wall in July 1963. The sign states 'End of the French sector' and the lower one 'Roadblock – the wall of shame'.

traps, watchtowers, mines, guard dogs, a further fence inside the GDR, and what became known as 'no-man's land' or 'the death strip' between.

The whole 'inner-German border' stretched through Germany separating the FRG and the GDR (see page 84). Neither the Western Allies' nor Soviet troops guarded the actual border. US, French and British troops were stationed further away in other parts of West Berlin, and, in the East, the wall and 'inner-German border' were guarded by GDR soldiers. GDR border troops themselves were liable to heavy prison sentences of up to five years if they did not prevent those who attempted the 'flight from the republic'. Those guards who did kill GDR citizens attempting to cross the border received honours, extra payments and even buildings or roads named after them; they became (in the East German government's eyes at least) national heroes.

The GDR devoted immense resources to the defence of the 'inner-German border' and the Berlin Wall. Around 50,000 border troops were deployed throughout its entire period, and the amount of equipment deployed in 1961 alone included is shown in Table 2.11.

Table 2.11: Resources deployed by the GDR on the 'inner-German border'

Resource	Number	Resource	Number
Tanks	60	Motorcycles	794
Wagons	374	Cars	1,221
Small guns	39,391	Trucks	1,365
Machine guns	5,554	Boats	2,035
Cannons	144		

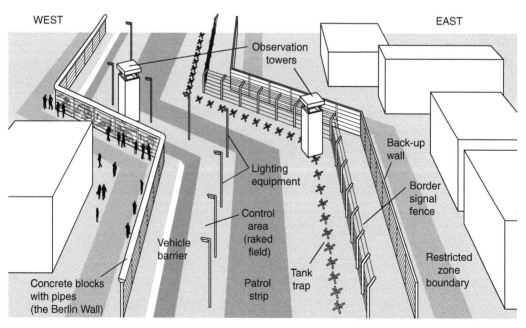

The Berlin Wall.

Escape attempts

There were some early escape attempts including jumping from windows, using hot-air balloons, and driving at full speed across the checkpoints. This last method was prevented by making the roads at the crossing points zig-zagged. Tunnels were also dug. All this led to the suppression in the GDR of certain sports activities which might help individuals to escape, such as hot-air ballooning or scuba diving. It is estimated that 5000 successfully escaped across the Berlin Wall between August 1961 and November 1989. However, 191 were killed at the border. Another 5000 are reckoned to have been held in GDR prisons by the mid-1970s for attempting 'flight from the republic', with prison sentences ranging from two to eight years.

Clearly, each of the individuals killed in attempting to cross the Berlin Wall or the 'inner-German border' represents a human tragedy. Two individuals, however, of particular note are Peter Fechter (1944–62) and Chris Gueffroy (1968–89). Fechter was a bricklayer from East Berlin. When he was 18 years old he tried to cross the Berlin Wall, but was shot by GDR border guards in front of hundreds of witnesses. Despite his screams no one from either the East or West came to his assistance. His slow bleeding to death was captured live on West German television. After a few

Peter Fechter, 18 years old, dying at the Berlin Wall very close to Checkpoint Charlie, 17 August 1962.

Table 2.12: Number of deaths at the 'inner-German border'

Place of death	Before 13 August 1961	13 August 1961 to 1989	Total
Berlin Wall	37	190	227
'Inner-German border'	247	237	484
Baltic Sea	17	164	181
Borders with Warsaw Pact nations	16	49	65
Others (e.g. transit routes, gliders, tunnels)	61	47	108
Total	378	687	1065

hours his body was taken away by GDR border guards. In 1990, a memorial was built at the spot where he died. The last person to be shot trying to cross the border was Chris Gueffroy on 6 February 1989. This was only 10 months before the actual opening of the Berlin Wall. The four East German border guards involved later won an award of RM150 each. Gueffroy was the only person shot trying to cross the wall whose death was reported in the GDR press. A monument was built to him in 2003 on what would have been his 35th birthday.

Communication between the GDR and the FRG

There were eight border crossings between East and West Berlin allowing access by West Berliners and West Germans, foreigners and Allied personnel into East Berlin. East German citizens could apply, especially old-age pensioners, to visit the West. Initially all crossing points were closed to West Berliners from the wall's construction until December 1963, when over Christmas and New Year more than a million West Berliners took advantage of being able to visit East Berlin. From 1964, old-age pensioners in the GDR could spend one four-week period per year visiting relatives in the FRG (official figures showed that less than 0.5 per cent failed to return to the GDR). On returning home many commented on the greed and lack of solidarity in the West. Travel restrictions were eased by a Four-Power Agreement in September 1971 (see page 80) on issuing passes that allowed West Germans to visit the GDR. Friedrichstrasse Station was a crossing point that West Berliners could use to visit East Berlin. It was known locally as 'the palace of tears' since it was so often the scene of East and West Germans greeting and saying goodbye to friends and relatives.

There were four motorways which West Germans could use to travel to and from West Berlin. The FRG had always paid the GDR to maintain them and by the 1980s this amounted to a lump sum from the FRG to the GDR of DM500 million. Access from West Germany to West Berlin was also possible by four railway routes and by canals and rivers. Western foreigners could legally cross the wall, and the East Germans welcomed their hard currency. They were always subject to careful checks on entering and leaving. The police would typically run a mirror under each vehicle to look for people clinging underneath. Westerners could also cross the border at **Checkpoint Charlie**. The building put up

Key question
How did communication between East and West Germany change?

Checkpoint Charlie
A crossing point between East and West Berlin. It was the only border crossing that could be used by both visitors and Allied forces. In the East it was called the Zimmermann Strasse border crossing.

at this crossing in the US zone remained a simple wooden building, demonstrating that the US expected it initially to be only a temporary requirement. In fact, it lasted for nearly 30 years, but to have put up a more permanent style building would have indicated acceptance of the wall.

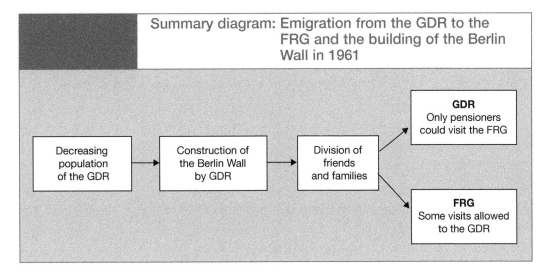

Summary diagram: Emigration from the GDR to the FRG and the building of the Berlin Wall in 1961

Study Guide: AS Question

In the style of Edexcel

How far do you agree that, for the GDR, the results of the building of the Berlin Wall proved to be mainly negative?

Exam tips

The cross-references are intended to take you straight to the material that will help you to answer the question.

In planning your answer to this question, keep the key words in mind. These are 'results' and 'mainly negative'. The question is asking you to evaluate the outcomes of this event. You will not need to explain the causes, but you should establish what indicators you are going to use to show 'negative' results. You should also find some positive outcomes and then consider which outweighs the other in order to address 'mainly' in the question.

The following might be termed negative outcomes, but you will have to show that their effects were in some way detrimental to the GDR:

- the human dimension; dividing friends and families (pages 65–6)
- the increased defence costs (page 68)
- the propaganda value for the West of a socialist state having to contain its people in this way (page 67).

The following might be termed positive effects, but you will have to show their benefit:

- the drain of skilled and valuable labour ended (page 66)
- better economic planning and progress resulted from the existence of a guaranteed labour supply (page 66)
- greater acceptance of, and co-operation with, government policies resulted from the lack of alternatives. The scale of emigration had previously called into question the legitimacy of the GDR (page 66).

You should reach an overall judgement rather than sit on the fence (or the wall). Your essay will flow better if you first deal with the argument you find weaker, and then marshal your evidence in support of the conclusion you intend to reach. This approach to essay planning could be described as 'building a wall in order to knock it down'!

Study Guide: A2 Question

In the style of AQA

How successful was the GDR's management of its economy between 1949 and 1964?

Exam tips

The cross-references are intended to take you straight to the material that will help you to answer the question.

In order to answer this question you will need to look at the table on page 63 and re-read the sections on agriculture and industry (pages 52–3). The material on emigration and the Berlin Wall (pages 60–2) is also relevant to the assessment here.

   You will need to explain the dates of the question as the years relating to the founding of the GDR and its acceptance as a member of COMECON. By 1964, the GDR could rightly claim to be the strongest Eastern bloc state, economically. In assessing this success, you will need to address:

• the command economy and the nationalisation of industry
• the collectivisation of agriculture
• GDR living standards
• the alignment of the GDR to the Eastern bloc countries
• emigration; the Berlin Wall and its economic effects to 1964.

Do not forget that the 'success' of the East German economy by 1964 needs also to be measured against contemporary economic development and living standards in the West, and you may wish to read sections of the next chapter in order to help with this.

3 Developments in the FRG 1969–88

POINTS TO CONSIDER

After a three-year period of federal government formed by the CDU and SPD in the 'Grand Coalition', Wily Brandt became the FRG's first SPD Chancellor in 1969. His *Ostpolitik* marked a significant turning point in West German foreign policy with its focus on developing relations between the FRG and the GDR and other states in the Eastern bloc.

The 1970s were challenging for the FRG. It faced economic problems, the emergence of left-wing terrorist activities and a younger generation that was often very critical of the FRG's handling of its recent past and the direction that they felt the FRG was taking both domestically and in foreign policy. The early 1980s then saw a period of international Cold War tension and widespread public opposition in the FRG to NATO's deployment of nuclear weapons on West German territory. The period of SPD domination of federal politics ended with Helmut Kohl becoming Chancellor of the FRG in 1982.

These issues will be examined through the following key themes:

- The leaders of the FRG 1969–88
- The development and impact of *Ostpolitik*
- The challenges facing the West German economy in the 1970s
- The growth of internal opposition and terrorism in the FRG

Key dates

1969	Brandt elected SPD Chancellor
1970	Visits between Brandt and GDR Chairman Stoph in the GDR and in the FRG
1972	Basic Treaty between the GDR and the FRG was signed
1973	Oil crisis began
1982	New coalition government led by Kohl (CDU/FDP)

1 | The Leaders of the FRG 1969–88

Key question
What were the
achievements of the
leaders of the FRG
between 1969 and
1988?

After the towering figure of Adenauer, and the success of his governments in rebuilding the FRG in the post-war period, the domestic achievements of the Chancellors who followed him are less remarkable. Of the three long-serving Chancellors, two of them, Brandt and Kohl, are chiefly remembered for the impact of their policies on relations with the 'other Germany'. Schmidt faced domestic challenges arguably greater than either of them (see pages 77 and 94–5), but his achievements in maintaining the stability and increasing the economic strength of the FRG in spite of them receive less acclaim.

Willy Brandt

Key dates

Brandt elected SPD
Chancellor: 1969

New coalition
government led by
Kohl (CDU/FDP):
1982

Ostpolitik won Brandt significant international acclaim, as well as widespread endorsement from the West German public, despite the reservations of a minority (see page 84). Brandt's success in the 1972 West German federal election marked the height of his political career. Afterwards his government faced growing economic challenges and a growth in terrorism. Overall, Brandt was less successful in dealing with domestic problems. One historian, Glees, has gone as far as to describe Brandt's

Table 3.1: Political developments in the FRG 1966–89

Chancellor and period in office	Political developments
Kurt Kiesinger 1966–9	In 1966 Erhard was replaced as Chancellor by Kiesinger's (CDU) 'Grand Coalition' with Willy Brandt (SPD) as Vice-Chancellor and Foreign Minister. This coalition government faced the end of the 'economic miracle' and the beginning of social unrest.
Willy Brandt 1969–74	Following Brandt's election in 1969, West German federal politics were dominated by the SPD until 1982.
Helmut Schmidt 1974–82	Schmidt succeeded Brandt as SPD Chancellor in 1974. He had played a key role in the modernisation of the SPD when it had adopted the Bad Godesberg programme in 1959 (see page 50). During this period, the Green Party grew as opposition gathered on issues such as the environment, nuclear power and rearmament, and attracted significant support from middle-class SPD supporters. The federal coalition government led by Schmidt collapsed in 1982 when the FDP switched its support from the SPD to the CDU.
Helmut Kohl 1982–90	In October 1982 the West German *Bundestag* supported a vote of no-confidence in Schmidt and voted for Kohl of the CDU/CSU as the new Chancellor. This was the first and, to date, the only time in the history of post-war Germany that a Chancellor has left office in this way. To counter some criticisms that he needed a mandate from the general public, Kohl wanted fresh elections as soon as was possible to demonstrate that he had popular support. The *Bundestag* was dissolved and Kohl went on to win the 1983 federal election.

Profile: Willy Brandt 1913–92

1913	– Born in Lübeck to a single mother
1930	– Joined the SPD
1933	– Left Germany for Norway to escape Nazi persecution
1945	– Worked as a journalist for a Scandinavian newspaper covering the Nuremberg Trials
1948	– Rejoined the SPD in West Berlin
1957–66	– Mayor of West Berlin
1966	– FRG Vice-Chancellor and Foreign Minister in the 'Grand Coalition'
1969	– First SPD Chancellor of the FRG
1971	– Won the Nobel Peace Prize for developing relations with the FRG and the Eastern bloc
1974	– Resigned after the Guillaume affair
1979–83	– Member of the European parliament
1987	– Retired as head of the SPD
1992	– Given a state funeral

In the 1969 West German federal election the SPD gained more than 40 per cent of the vote and Brandt became the first West German SPD Chancellor, with a government formed in coalition with the FDP. He was also seen as a 'good German' as he had fought with the Norwegian resistance against the Nazis during the Second World War. This, together with his relatively humble background, made him particularly popular with the younger generation who wanted the FRG to move towards a more liberal and less hierarchical state. The replacement of many of the older, more authoritarian government figures was seen by many as the beginning of a period of renewal and change.

Brandt's first speech as Chancellor in the *Bundestag* had ended with the phrase 'Let's dare more democracy!' Brandt wanted reforms in education and in social welfare provision and a lowering of the voting age in an attempt to overcome what he saw as the alienation of many of the younger generation from mainstream politics. His main achievements were undoubtedly in West German foreign policy. He particularly wanted far more accommodation with, and improved relations between, the FRG and the GDR, as well as with the other states in the Eastern bloc and the USSR. His *Ostpolitik* (see page 80) had a lasting impact on West German politics and formed the basis for further work by Schmidt and Kohl, the West German Chancellors who succeeded him. Brandt's work on developing the FRG's international relations was recognised when he won the Nobel Peace Prize in 1971. He was also the first West German Chancellor to visit Israel, in 1973. As a tribute to Brandt, when the SPD moved its headquarters from Bonn to Berlin following reunification, its central office was named 'Willy Brandt House'. He was also the first major left-of-centre West German politician to argue for German reunification, in late 1989.

It was neither the economic recession (see page 87) nor the emergence of terrorism (see pages 91 and 94) that brought Brandt's Chancellorship to a sudden end. In 1974, one of Brandt's major advisers, Günter Guillaume, was discovered to be a GDR spy who was directly reporting to Markus Wolf, head of the *Stasi*'s foreign intelligence section. To make matters worse for Brandt, he had apparently been aware for several months that Guillaume was under suspicion but had not acted on this knowledge. This led to Brandt's resignation as Chancellor, although he remained chairman of the SPD itself. Wolf stated after the reunification of Germany that Brandt's resignation had never been intended, and that the affair had been one of the biggest mistakes of the East German secret service.

Chancellorship as 'a shambles' and to suggest that he managed to survive only by a combination of personal charisma, the lack of an alternative, and the success of the FRG's political system.

Helmut Schmidt

Schmidt's Chancellorship was dominated by economic problems, although in many ways the FRG dealt better than other nations with the problems caused by the world oil crisis in the mid-1970s (see page 87). Schmidt maintained good international relations with the USA, oversaw some economic recovery and continued Brandt's *Ostpolitik*. He remained as Chancellor in a coalition government with the FDP after elections in 1976 and 1980. He won significant support from the West German public over his handling of the hijacking of a German airliner by terrorists in 1977 (see page 94).

However, renewed economic problems resulting from the second oil crisis (see page 88), and the impending deployment of nuclear weapons in the FRG led to Schmidt's increasing unpopularity.

Helmut Kohl

Kohl was keen to continue further integration with Western Europe. He developed particularly close relations with France. This included a symbolic meeting with the French President Mitterrand at the site of the First World War battle at Verdun in France to commemorate soldiers from both sides killed during the First and Second World Wars. As well as displaying French–German reconciliation, this meeting formed the basis for later political and economic co-operation on EU projects such as the Maastricht Treaty and the introduction of the euro. In addition to developing the FRG's relations with the West, Kohl displayed a commitment to the *Ostpolitik* followed by the two former SPD Chancellors. This included the symbolic visit to the FRG by Honecker in 1987, the first state visit by a GDR leader to the FRG. Kohl also developed closer contact between the FRG and the USA from the mid-1980s, and also with the USSR after

Gorbachev's rise to power. These developments were to play a key role in the process of German reunification between 1989 and 1990 (see Chapter 5).

The extent of the FRG's achievements by 1989

the FRG had made remarkable post-war recovery, and its successful overcoming of both economic challenges and internal left-wing opposition demonstrated that it had become a stable, well-functioning democracy. It had demonstrated the effectiveness of its new democratic political institutions.

However, various social and economic trends undermined its claims to have become a 'model democracy'. The increased government and police powers in response to rising opposition imposed some restrictions on individual liberties. The concept of the FRG as a 'model democracy' was also challenged by the social and economic inequalities faced by the guest workers (see page 88).

This photograph shows West German Chancellor Kohl (right) and French President Mitterrand (left) at the memorial service at Verdun in September 1984.

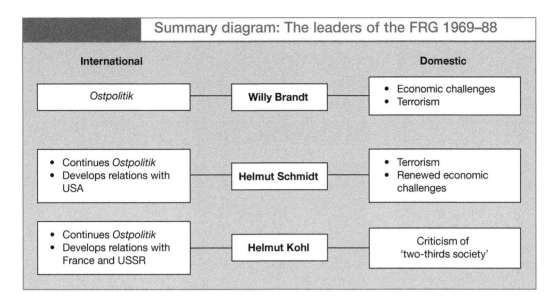

Summary diagram: The leaders of the FRG 1969–88

International

| | | **Domestic** |

Ostpolitik — **Willy Brandt** — • Economic challenges / • Terrorism

• Continues *Ostpolitik*
• Develops relations with USA — **Helmut Schmidt** — • Terrorism / • Renewed economic challenges

• Continues *Ostpolitik*
• Develops relations with France and USSR — **Helmut Kohl** — Criticism of 'two-thirds society'

2 | The Development and Impact of *Ostpolitik*

The principles and early stages of *Ostpolitik*

Key question
What were the main aims of *Ostpolitik*?

Brandt's earlier years as mayor of West Berlin during the construction of the Berlin Wall were a powerful influence on him. He had been very critical of how long it had taken for Chancellor Adenauer to visit Berlin in August 1961 after the construction of the wall. In a major shift of West German foreign policy, Brandt wanted the FRG to develop relations with the East and reduce the negative effects of Germany's division. Chief among his diplomatic strengths was his capacity to take the FRG in small steps in the direction he wanted it to go. He was a pragmatist and a realist. It was evident in his reference in Moscow in August 1970 to 'the political situation as it exists in Europe' that he was prepared to acknowledge the current *de facto* division of Germany as part of a move to reduce that divide. However, he believed that his policy of *Ostpolitik* would eventually undermine the existence of a separate socialist East Germany.

Brandt argued that Adenauer's foreign policy had always looked towards the West and that the FRG should now follow a foreign policy which looked towards improving relations not just with the GDR, but with the entire Eastern bloc. This was to become a key feature and a long-lasting legacy of Brandt's governments after he first became Chancellor in 1969. In essence, *Ostpolitik* aimed to develop relations between the FRG and the GDR with a policy of '*rapprochement*' rather than a policy of strength (see pages 30 and 40). It was very controversial and there was significant opposition from much of the CDU, from some of Brandt's own SPD and from many of the public. *Ostpolitik* was only possible because of a thaw in superpower relations between the USA and the USSR following the **Cuban Missile Crisis** and the consequent emergence of the policy of *détente*.

Key terms

Rapprochement
Developing contact and relations by diplomacy and agreement.

Cuban Missile Crisis
A serious confrontation in 1962 between the USA and the USSR after Soviet nuclear bases were found to have been installed in Cuba.

In March 1970 Willy Brandt met Willi Stoph (leader of the GDR's Council of Ministers) in Erfurt in the GDR. This was the first ever meeting between senior government figures of the FRG and GDR and demonstrated that measures to develop better mutual relations were being taken very seriously by both Germanys. The attitude of the East German public was evident in the enthusiastic public welcome which Brandt received. Brandt was greeted with large crowds of excited East German citizens lining the streets with banners displaying a big 'Y' to show it was Willy Brandt rather than Willi Stoph that they were cheering for. The crowds were much smaller and less enthusiastic for Stoph's return visit to the FRG in May 1970. The East German government was taken aback at the amount of popular support shown for Brandt.

The East German authorities were determined that such embarrassment would not reoccur and they made careful plans for the next visit by a West German Chancellor. When Chancellor Schmidt visited the GDR in December 1981, the visit was very carefully stage-managed. The East German authorities ensured that the streets were cleared. The *Stasi* ordered any members of the local population they considered be unreliable to stay at home. Other loyal East German citizens were transported in especially for the occasion. However, the West German delegation did remark that some supposedly local people who were present did not have the expected local accents.

Key dates

Visits between Brandt and GDR Chairman Stoph in the GDR and in the FRG: 1970

Basic Treaty between the GDR and the FRG was signed: 1972

The development of relations between the FRG and the GDR

Key question
How did *Ostpolitik* develop?

Ostpolitik led to a series of agreements which addressed some of the key foreign policy issues and improved relations between the FRG and the Eastern bloc. These are listed in Table 3.2.

In the early 1970s these developments were possible because of both domestic and international factors. The FRG had in Brandt a new SPD Chancellor committed to a change in West German foreign policy. The GDR leader Ulbricht was replaced by Honecker in 1971, who was keen to develop the GDR's own identity separate from that of the FRG's. These changes provoked opposition within the FRG, since they involved acceptance of many unpopular aspects of the post-war settlement, however

Table 3.2: Agreements leading from the *Ostpolitik* policy

Agreement	Terms
Treaty of Moscow 1970	The FRG and the USSR agreed that they had no territorial claims against each other.
Treaty of Warsaw 1970	The FRG agreed to respect Poland's western border with the GDR – the Oder–Neisse line.
The Four-Power Treaty 1971	The GDR would allow access from the FRG to West Berlin, and West Berliners would be able to visit East Berlin. This treaty is sometimes referred to as the 'Berlin accord'.
The Basic Treaty 1972	Both the FRG and the GDR agreed to develop normal relations, to recognise each other's existence, and settle any differences without the threat or use of force.

Solidarity
An anti-socialist trade union, which began in Poland in the early 1980s and influenced the growth of reform movements throughout Eastern Europe.

What was the significance of the Basic Treaty?

Warsaw Ghetto
The largest Jewish ghetto in Nazi-occupied Europe. Between 1940 and 1943 a large proportion of its half a million inhabitants died from disease or starvation or were transported to Nazi extermination camps.

Why was *Ostpolitik* so controversial?

Brandt's success in the election of 1972 indicated a majority endorsement of *Ostpolitik*. In particular, the Basic Treaty seemed to indicate that a divided Germany was now permanent.

An important feature of continuity throughout the period of *Ostpolitik* was the FRG's Foreign Minister from 1974 to 1992, Hans-Dietrich Genscher. He played a major role in developing *Ostpolitik* and is widely respected for his efforts at ending the Cold War and the reuniting of Germany. He met the Polish **Solidarity** leader, Lech Walesa, in early 1988, and also addressed crowds of East German refugees at the West German embassy in Prague in September 1989.

The significance of the 1972 Basic Treaty

The agreement of the FRG and the GDR formally to recognise each other's existence had a significance far beyond formalities. The Basic Treaty was the foundation for the development of relationships between the two Germanys. As well as developing inter-German relations it reduced some wider international Cold War tensions:

- It did much to reduce the threat of conflict over West Berlin.
- It reinforced previous agreements giving West Berliners access to East Berlin, which was obviously of great personal significance for those divided by the wall from friends and family.
- It meant greater international recognition of the GDR.
- It made it possible for both the GDR and the FRG to become members of the United Nations in 1973.

However, the FRG still did not acknowledge the GDR as a separate foreign state under international law. East German citizens could still claim West German citizenship automatically. There were no West German or East German ambassadors in either of the two Germanys. Instead they had 'representatives'. The FRG still formally stated in its constitution that it was committed to the eventual reuniting of both Germanys.

Arguments surrounding *Ostpolitik*

Ostpolitik caused much controversy. During a visit to Poland in December 1970, Brandt spontaneously knelt down at the memorial for the victims of Nazism in the **Warsaw Ghetto**. This action was widely interpreted as the FRG seeking forgiveness and wanting to work towards post-war reconciliation. However, although international opinion generally admired Brandt's symbolic act, within the FRG he faced fierce criticism, especially from those Germans who had lost their homes in territory that had become part of Poland following the Second World War. Table 3.3 (see page 85) summarises the arguments for and against *Ostpolitik*.

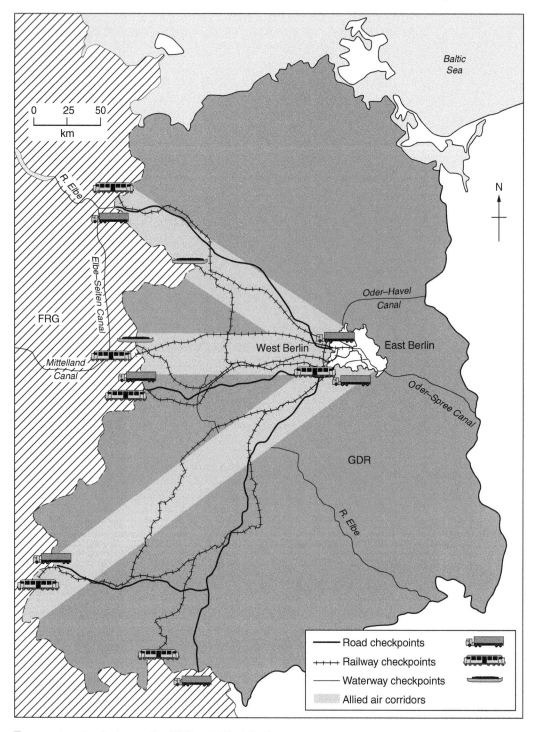

Transport routes between the FRG and West Berlin.

The West German Chancellor, Willy Brandt, kneeling at the Monument to the Warsaw Ghetto in Warsaw, December 1970.

Key question
How did *Ostpolitik*
influence the division
of Germany?

The impact of *Ostpolitik*

A significant area of debate is whether *Ostpolitik* actually helped to create the necessary conditions leading towards the eventual reunification of Germany or whether it sustained the division of the two Germanys:

- On the one hand, the principle of establishing and developing relations between the two Germanys was a process begun by Brandt, and continued by both Chancellors Schmidt and Kohl until the reuniting of the FRG and the GDR in 1990. Even at times of wider Cold War tension, such as in the early 1980s, both Germanys seemed intent on pursuing their own 'local' *détente*. It also gave the GDR a considerable economic advantage; from 1972 to 1989, the GDR received loans of nearly DM15 billion.
- On the other hand, two very different Germanys were becoming increasingly distinct. The GDR developed its own separate identity and it became known officially as 'The Workers' and Peasants' State'. The two Germanys continued to develop along very different political, social and economic lines and the increasing psychological division of the people was also becoming more apparent.
- Although the West German constitution was still formally committed to reunification, the division of Germany was increasingly viewed by the majority of politicians and the general public as the accepted status quo. The debate on

The 'inner-German border' from the eastern side in Thuringia in 1971. The border was up to 5 km wide and included mines, fences and watchtowers.

reunification was, according to Fulbrook, 'simply a sacred cow to which lip-service could be paid while recognising the reality, and likely permanence, of division'. Overall, there was a growing acceptance of Germany's division. Discussion of the reuniting of Germany became increasingly low on the political agenda of the major political parties in the FRG, and most of the opinion polls in the FRG showed a gradual trend towards the acceptance of Germany's division. In fact, an increasing number in the FRG were actually becoming opposed to the idea of German reunification.

• There were still strains in the relationship between the two Germanys. The FRG continued to criticise the GDR government for its abuse of human rights. The relationship between the two Germanys was also subject to the vicissitudes in superpower relations. Despite the development of *Ostpolitik*, both sides still kept up with preparations for the possibility of nuclear war, which included the construction of a new nuclear shelter in West Berlin in 1973 capable of accommodating 27,000 people.

International recognition of the GDR through sport

Participation in international sports events was heavily promoted by both Ulbricht and Honecker. It would reduce the GDR's international isolation, and develop national pride within the GDR itself. During the 1950s and early 1960s, East German sports representatives participated in international events as part of an all-German team, but from the 1964 Tokyo Olympics onwards, sportsmen and sportswomen were part of a separate

Key question
How did sporting links develop the GDR's status?

Table 3.3: Arguments against and for *Ostpolitik*

	Opposition to Ostpolitik	*Support for* Ostpolitik
In parliament	Many MPs argued that the 1972 Basic Treaty showed the FRG's acceptance and, to some extent, approval of the GDR. They argued that giving up aspects of the Hallstein Doctrine would ultimately lead towards the permanent division of Germany. The CDU were predominantly against *Ostpolitik*, as were some of Brandt's own SPD. The SPD also lost much of its traditional support from refugees in the FRG.	Although Brandt lost some support from his own political party, there was closer co-operation between his own SPD Party and the FDP in federal politics. There were also some CDU MPs who supported Brandt, although it was discovered that since the reunification of Germany some had actually accepted financial bribes from the *Stasi* to vote in favour of *Ostpolitik*. Brandt argued that *Ostpolitik* was not about accepting Germany's division but was a means of keeping the issue very much alive by developing discussion and negotiation.
Public opinion	Many West German conservatives of the older generation were also opposed to what they saw as the FRG's agreeing to the loss of German territory that had become part of Poland in 1945. Those Germans who had been expelled from former German territories in the east went as far as to argue that the *Ostpolitik* was illegal, some even describing it as treason.	Supporters of *Ostpolitik* argued that it was a much more pragmatic approach, which would provide for greater personal contact between the two Germanys – something that many of the divided population obviously welcomed. There was support from the younger generation in particular, as well as from many prominent West German left-wing intellectuals.
The 1972 federal election with *Ostpolitik* the single most important issue	A federal election was held in 1972 owing to Brandt's losing the support of some members who were opposed to *Ostpolitik*.	The result was the best ever federal election result for the SPD; Brandt remained as Chancellor for a second term. The turnout had also been very high. This result indicated widespread public support for the continuation of his *Ostpolitik*.

GDR team, and, from 1968, the GDR had its own separate national flag and anthem. In the 1968 Olympic Games in Mexico, the GDR finished in third place after the USA and the USSR in the medals table. Throughout its history, the GDR achieved impressive results in many Olympic Games events and it won far more medals than the FRG. Table 3.4 shows the five highest scoring states in the 1972 Munich Olympic Games.

Table 3.4: Medals gained in the 1972 Munich Olympic Games

Country	Gold	Silver	Bronze
USSR	50	27	22
USA	33	31	30
GDR	20	23	23
FRG	13	11	16
Japan	13	8	16

This success was partly due to the very heavy promotion of sport generally within the GDR. Sport was seen as a necessary part of keeping generations healthy for national defence, and more talented young people were developed at an early age at the GDR's élite sports schools, which were offering 10,000 places by 1989. Such places included significant opportunities for individuals to be able to travel abroad as well as being paid in Western currency. However, sporting competitions were viewed by the GDR in military and Cold War ideological terms, as a fight against Western 'imperialist enemies'. The GDR's participants in the 1972 Munich Olympics were officially briefed not to have contact with athletes from capitalist states.

Since the reuniting of Germany, it has been discovered that many top sports representatives from the GDR were subjected to excessive amounts of performance-enhancing drugs and hormone treatment, which left many with long-term health problems.

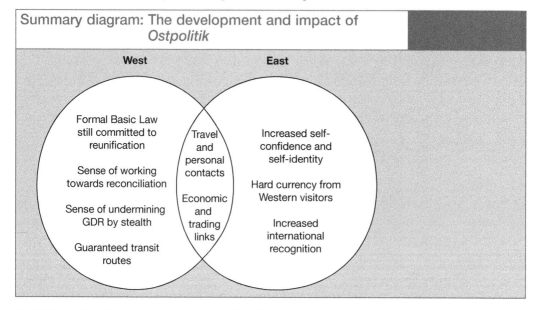

Summary diagram: The development and impact of *Ostpolitik*

West

Formal Basic Law still committed to reunification

Sense of working towards reconciliation

Sense of undermining GDR by stealth

Guaranteed transit routes

Travel and personal contacts

Economic and trading links

East

Increased self-confidence and self-identity

Hard currency from Western visitors

Increased international recognition

3 | The Challenges Facing the West German Economy in the 1970s and 1980s

The West German economy in the 1970s

Overall, the 'economic miracle' of the post-war period meant that the West German economy was still powerful and, in many ways, better able to withstand the economic challenges during the 1970s than much of Europe. Some explanations of this focus on a number of unquantifiable features, such as the attitude and disposition of the workforce, a national determination to work hard, and fear of the consequences of economic crises. Many Germans still had memories of the troubles which had devastated Germany in the 1920s and 1930s. Other explanations emphasise the success of well-developed industrial relations and management techniques, and remark on the contribution to the economy of low-paid guest workers who did vital, yet unsavoury jobs, shunned by many West Germans.

Key question
What problems began to face the West German economy in the 1970s?

Under Erhard's government, there were already clear indications that the 'economic miracle' was coming to an end with a combination of falling economic growth and rising unemployment. Discontent was surfacing. Some trade unions were demanding higher wages. There was concern at the neo-Nazi NPD party's gaining seats in some state elections; it won up to 10 per cent of the vote in Bavaria and in Baden-Württemberg in 1968. Much more challenging though, was the growth in left-wing opposition from the student movement (see pages 90–1). Brandt's government had passed a series of social welfare reforms, such as increases in unemployment allowances and pensions, better public health insurance, and more financial support for students from lower income backgrounds. However, this was obviously increasing government spending, which, together with rising inflation, was putting strains on the national economy. Some government members began voicing alarm at the increasing levels of public expenditure. Between 1969 and 1972, the education budget had more than doubled, and welfare expenditure had risen from DM17 billion to DM22 billion.

Key date
Oil crisis began: 1973

The 1973 oil crisis

Key question
What was the significance of the 1973 oil crisis for the FRG?

The economy of the FRG was seriously affected by the 1973 oil crisis. In 1973, **OPEC** trebled the price of oil, which was in part a response to the USA's action in supplying Israel's armed forces during the **Yom Kippur War**. This led to increasing costs of other raw materials. Government measures to deal with the problem were unpopular. To reduce oil consumption, the federal government introduced car-free Sundays and, for the first time ever imposed speed limits on West German motorways. By 1974, inflation was over five per cent and unemployment levels had reached three million. High unemployment brought three interlinked problems: falling revenues from taxation, rising public expenditure and rising rates of taxation on those in work. The high unemployment levels were exacerbated by the demographic increase in younger people. The post-war '**baby boom**' created a demand for nearly 100,000 jobs a year. Rising job shortages also led to increasing resentment and hostility towards the guest workers and there were even calls for them to be expelled from the FRG. This led to a ban on further recruitment of foreign workers in 1973, although guest worker numbers in the FRG were still growing as many were being joined by their families. Nevertheless, compared to other Western economies, the West German economy in the mid- to late 1970s under Helmut Schmidt proved to be much more resilient. There were several reasons for this.

Key terms

OPEC
Organisation of Petroleum Exporting Counties: a largely Middle Eastern oil cartel.

Yom Kippur War
Also known as the Fourth Arab–Israeli War, when Egypt and Syria led a largely unsuccessful attack against Israel in October 1973.

Baby boom
The sudden increase in the post-war birth rate. By the early 1970s those born in immediate post-war years were of working age.

Underlying economic strengths
- The West German economy managed to maintain a high level of exports. German goods continued to be in demand internationally owing to their high quality. Throughout the mid-1970s, export businesses continued to take on workers.
- Many West German businesses showed a high level of marketing and advertising skills which helped to open up

international markets to German goods. Major West German companies continued to be willing to risk investment in major projects within their own country.

Government decisions

- As a result of the oil crisis, Schmidt became more determined to solve any future energy crises by developing the FRG's commitment to the use of nuclear energy. This economic policy, however, had serious political repercussions for Schmidt. It created increasing opposition for him from his own SPD in the *Bundestag*.
- With French President Giscard d'Estaing, Schmidt began to take a lead in developing the European Monetary System. This co-ordination of EEC monetary systems also helped economic recovery and a reduction in unemployment.

The 'two-thirds society'

In the later 1970s there was an overall trend of wage increases and falling unemployment until the second oil crisis hit in 1979–80. This sent the economy back into recession in the early 1980s. Unemployment rose and led to concerns about the development of a 'two-thirds society'. This referred to the situation in which a section of the working-age population at around two million people remained long-term unemployed. This other 'third of society' included a disproportionately high number of guest workers whom left-wingers claimed were neglected by the West German government.

Helmut Kohl's first Chancellorship was dominated by the economic situation. Kohl immediately embarked on a policy of cutting government expenditure on welfare provision. Inflation fell to two per cent by 1983, and a drop in oil prices in the mid-1980s helped the West German economy to recover by the later 1980s.

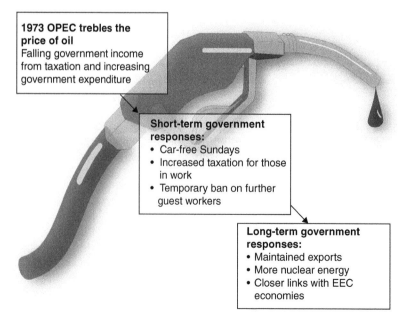

1973 OPEC trebles the price of oil
Falling government income from taxation and increasing government expenditure

Short-term government responses:
- Car-free Sundays
- Increased taxation for those in work
- Temporary ban on further guest workers

Long-term government responses:
- Maintained exports
- More nuclear energy
- Closer links with EEC economies

The 1973 oil crisis and its effects on the FRG.

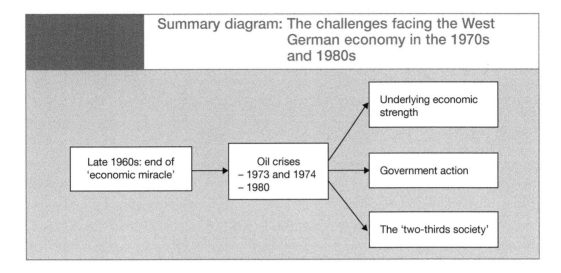

Summary diagram: The challenges facing the West German economy in the 1970s and 1980s

4 | The Growth of Internal Opposition and Terrorism in the FRG

Youth opposition and the APO

Youth

Key question
Why did so much opposition from the young emerge in the 1960s?

The economic miracle had contributed to the development of a new youth culture as many young people could now afford to live away from home, and the economic miracle had funded the expansion of higher education. Many young West Germans eagerly accepted US popular culture such as rock music, films and fashion, although some organisations opposed what they saw as a threatening dilution of the German language with American vocabulary. The mid to late 1960s saw the emergence of strong opposition to the West German government from the younger generation. This was based on issues similar to those arousing

Table 3.5: The range of issues leading to protest in the FRG from the mid-1960s

Opposition relating to general and international issues	*Opposition relating to issues specific to the FRG*
Questioning of US policies and the FRG's increasing political ties to the USA. The FRG was seen to be supporting US military involvement in Vietnam.	The preoccupation of many West Germans with materialism and consumerism.
The increasing military spending by both NATO and the Warsaw Pact and the proliferation of nuclear weapons.	The FRG's failure to 'denazify'. The issue was highlighted by Eichmann's trial in Jerusalem and the second Auschwitz trials.
Many of the issues that the younger generation were demonstrating about in the 1960s were identical to those in other Western nations and the USA, such as equality for all, regardless of race or gender.	Fears that membership of NATO would lead to the deployment of nuclear weapons on German soil.
	Frustration with the general reluctance to confront the recent past. Many young protestors challenged their parents with slogans such as 'What did you do in the war, daddy?'

protest in many other parts of Western Europe, as well as some opposition to issues specific to the FRG. Widespread protests over the issues shown in Table 3.5 continued from the late 1960s until the mid-1970s.

The APO

The opposition was initially organised by APO ('Opposition Outside of Parliament'), a loose grouping of left-wing students and trade unions which saw radical protest as the only way to challenge the *Bundestag* and achieve the setting up of a new West German Communist Party.

In 1966, more than 90 per cent of the West German *Bundestag* was controlled by the 'Grand Coalition'. Critics saw this as the unhealthy domination of federal politics by the SPD and the CDU, the two major political parties. The APO was formed with the aim of generating protest and political activity by organising strikes, marches and demonstrations. For those on the left this was seen as necessary in order to make the FRG more open and less conservative. However, by the late 1960s, membership of the APO started to decline:

- Many members of APO who had campaigned about the Grand Coalition's existence (and Chancellor Kiesinger's previous membership of the Nazi Party) joined mainstream politics by supporting the SPD when Brandt became Chancellor.
- Some joined the new West German Communist Party.
- Some joined the growing Green Party, which took away some of the middle-class support for the SPD and which was to make a significant impact within federal politics from the mid-1980s onwards.
- A few joined the emerging terrorist groups. The most noticeable of these was the Red Army Faction (RAF) (or the Baader–Meinhof Gang as it was known), which began operating in the early 1970s.

The German Socialist Students Union (SDS) and the 1968 movement

The SDS had originally been set up as the student section of the mainstream SPD Party in 1946. However, the SDS was opposed to the FRG's rearmament and in 1961 the SPD excluded any members of the SDS from joining the political party. The SDS ended a long period of conservatism among Germany's students and was a significant shift to radical student politics. From 1965 it was led by **Rudi Dutschke**. From the mid-1960s the SDS campaigned against the Vietnam War and the possession of nuclear weapons. It also protested against former Nazis holding influential positions within the FRG. The main methods of protest included sit-ins at universities and mass demonstrations. In 1967, during a student protest in West Berlin against an official state visit by the Shah of Iran, a student, Benno Ohnesorg, was shot dead by a police officer. This was followed by violent protests at most West German universities. The SDS reached a

Key figure

Rudi Dutschke 1940–79
Dutschke fled from East Berlin to West Berlin just one day before the construction of the Berlin Wall. Following Ohnesorg's death he warned against the SDS from becoming more violent and instead he argued that radical change in West German society needed a 'long march through the institutions of power'.

Table 3.6: The West German government's responses to the growth of opposition and terrorism

Year	Response
1968	The so-called 'Emergency Laws' were passed by the *Bundestag*, which meant that the federal government could, with a two-thirds majority, obtain any extra powers it felt were needed in times of a 'national emergency'.
1972	A new federal law barred 'radicals' from public sector employment. These included teachers, civil servants, postal workers and railway staff. Some estimates suggest that thousands of individuals were barred from public-sector employment because of their left-wing connections. It appeared the FRG was moving in a more authoritarian direction.
1973	As terrorism grew, the *Bundestag* saw no alternative but to treat those convicted of terrorism more harshly. Imprisoned members of the Red Army Faction had long periods of solitary confinement and were allowed visits only from government officials or prison chaplains.
1977	By 1977, the West German police listed nearly five million West Germans as sympathisers or supporters of terrorism and there were over 6000 individuals under police surveillance.

This photograph shows a demonstration against the 'Emergency Laws' in May 1968. The banner reads 'No *Reich*'.

peak of membership in 1968 when 80,000 students demonstrated in Bonn against the Emergency Legislation (see Table 3.6). However, the *Bundestag*'s passing of these laws and the death of Ohnesorg divided the student movement and overall led to its decline. Some were pushed towards more radical action which led to the setting up of the RAF. Others were against this move towards extremism and feared that it would only harm the student movement.

Concerns about the rise of extremism in the FRG

Some West Germans saw these developments as potential threats to the economically and politically successful state that the post-war FRG had become. They also brought back memories for older West Germans of the rise of Nazism. There were also fears that the *Stasi* were training and funding left-wing groups operating in the FRG; fears which were shown to have been correct when new information became available after the reunification of Germany in 1990. But alarm in the West German public at large and within the government, became very pronounced with the emergence of widespread terrorism from the early 1970s onwards. Although some of the federal government's responses may appear rather panic-stricken, the appearance of domestic terrorism shook a relatively newly formed state and recalled painful memories of the past.

The West German government's responses to increasing opposition and terrorism

As domestic opposition increased in a variety of forms, so did federal government action. Both Chancellors Brandt and Schmidt followed a firm line and strengthened government and police powers. Table 3.6 shows the West German government's responses to the growth of opposition and terrorism.

Terrorism in the FRG
The Munich Olympics 1972

In 1972 the FRG hosted the Olympic Games in Munich. The West German government hoped the event would help to override memories of when the last Olympic Games held in Germany in Berlin in 1936 had been used for Nazi propaganda purposes. The FRG was also particularly sensitive as many of the Israeli Olympic team had lost family in the Holocaust, and the site of the Olympics was very near to the former Nazi concentration camp at Dachau. During the games, members of the Israeli team were taken hostage by eight Palestinian terrorists demanding the release of over 200 Palestinian prisoners being held in Israeli prisons.

During the rescue attempt by the West German police, the Israeli hostages were all killed, as well as five of the terrorists. Although the Olympic Games resumed the following day, the events increased West German security and led to the FRG government's reassessing its approach to handling terrorism. As a consequence of the events at the Munich Olympics, the FRG created GSG9, a special élite force to combat terrorism.

The Red Army Faction (RAF)

The radical student protest movement led to the formation of the RAF, which was mainly made up of educated middle-class young people. It is more commonly referred to as the Baader–Meinhof Gang from the names of two of its most prominent members (Andreas Baader and Ulrike Meinhof), although the group never used this name themselves. This was a militant left-wing group which was responsible for a series of terrorist activities from 1970 to

Key question
How did the West German government deal with the threat of terrorism?

Key question
What were the consequences of the Munich Olympics 1972?

Key question
What led to the emergence of the RAF?

1993, although it did not officially disband until 1998. It initially carried out a series of bank robberies, and politically motivated bomb attacks, but became increasingly violent with kidnappings and murders, with a particularly intense period in late 1977 which has become known as the 'German autumn' (see page 94).

Initially, the RAF seemed to have a surprisingly high level of public support. Some West German opinion polls in the early 1970s suggested that around 15 per cent of the public supported their aims. But once the RAF's activities changed from bank robberies and arson attacks to the murdering of individuals, the vast majority condemned their actions. However, there was some criticism of the sensationalist reporting of the RAF by certain sections of the West German press, for example the West German

This wanted poster shows Ulrike Meinhof and Andreas Baader on the top left. The poster offers rewards of up to DM100,000 for information and ends with the statement 'Beware! These violent criminals will use guns ruthlessly!'

right-wing tabloid *Das Bild*. There was also concern at the increasing government and police powers. One response was Heinrich Böll's famous short story *The Lost Honour of Katharina Blum*, which tells the story of an innocent young woman who unknowingly meets a terrorist at a party and then becomes subjected to police raids on her home, intense interrogation and a very misinformed media campaign.

Table 3.7 shows a summary of major terrorist activities in the FRG.

Table 3.7: Terrorist incidents in the FRG 1968–85

Year	Incident
1968	Andreas Baader and Gudrun Enslinn (a leading member of the RAF) fire-bombed two department stores in Frankfurt. Baader was imprisoned, but managed to escape with the help of a left-wing journalist, Ulrike Meinhof.
1970	Several members of the RAF went to Jordan where they received training from the Palestinian Liberation Organisation. This was followed by a series of bank robberies and bombings in the FRG.
1971	Seven million copies of the wanted poster (see photograph on page 93) appeared in the FRG.
1972	Two staff at the West German embassy in Stockholm were killed. Five RAF members, including Baader and Meinhof, were arrested and placed in solitary confinement at Stammheim Prison, near Stuttgart. Those in prison went on hunger strike and had to be force-fed. Three died in prison, including Ulrike Meinhof, who hanged herself with a rope made from prison towels. The official investigation concluded that she had committed suicide but this did not prevent conspiracy theories from arising. In response to Meinhof's death there was a second wave of terrorism by other RAF members.
1973	The trial of three RAF members in prison was concluded. They were sentenced to life imprisonment for murder and attempted murder.
1977 (the 'German autumn')	West German chief public prosecutor Siegfried Buback was murdered. The chief executive of Dresdner Bank, Jurgen Ponto, was murdered at home. Head of the German Association of Employers, Hans Shleyer (a former Nazi member) was kidnapped. Arab supporters with RAF links hijacked a German plane heading from Majorca to Frankfurt, which was then flown to Mogadishu in Somalia. Schmidt refused to give into any of their demands, which included the release of RAF prisoners. This tough line won him widespread support from the West German public. Élite police force commandos stormed the plane, killed three of the hijackers and freed the hostages. The very same night that the news was broadcast in the FRG, three imprisoned RAF members, including Baader, were found dead in their prison cells. Baader had gunshot wounds and a range of conspiracy theories developed about how this could have happened. A later investigation stated that the RAF's lawyers could have smuggled guns in. Later in 1994, one of the RAF members when released from prison claimed that the deaths were organised by the West German government. The events of 1977 were later made into a television series called *Death Game*.
1979	The RAF attempted to assassinate the US Commander-in-Chief of NATO, Alexander Haig.
1985	A series of bombings to support imprisoned RAF members on hunger strike led to the assassination of the West German armaments industry executive, Ernst Zimmermann.
1986	Bombing at the US airforce base in Frankfurt killed two people. Siemens executive Karl Beckurts and his driver were killed in a car-bombing.
1998	The opening of the Berlin Wall in 1989 and the subsequent reuniting of Germany significantly weakened the group. In 1998 a letter signed 'RAF' was sent to a news agency and stated that the group was dissolved. A major factor was clearly the loss of the financial support that they had previously received from the GDR's *Stasi*.

Key question
What new political parties emerged in the FRG in the early 1980s?

New political parties
The rise of neo-Nazi organisations

Although the RAF's activities had significantly declined by the late 1980s, a major concern for the FRG was the rise of neo-Nazi organizations. In the late 1960s, there were fears that the far-right NPD would make gains in federal elections. It had already gained seats in some state parliaments in the late 1960s, such as Bavaria and Schleswig-Holstein and the Rhineland, but it had failed to gain sufficient support to get anywhere near the constitutional five per cent threshold that would have given it seats in the *Bundestag*.

However, in 1983, the Republikaner Party, a new extreme right-wing political party, was formed. Unlike the majority of members of the RAF who were predominantly from middle-class and educated backgrounds, far-right groups attracted mainly unskilled, low-educated and frequently unemployed supporters. They focused particular resentment and violence on the guest workers, and were initially led by Franz Schönhuber, a former member of the SS. In 1980 they gained representation in the European parliament and in the West German state parliament of Baden-Württemberg. These gains were lost by 2001 and the party became marginalised.

A new West German Communist Party

Adenauer's government had banned the West German Communist Party in 1966 following its support for the GDR and the USSR in their suppression of the 1953 June uprising. The emergence of left-wing opposition within the FRG can be seen in the establishment of a new West German Communist Party (DKP) in 1968, which received financial contributions from the GDR. It did, however, remain very much on the fringes of West German politics with a membership of only some 50,000, and very little support in either federal or state elections.

The Green Party enters the West German *Bundestag*

The growth of the Green Party was closely linked to the issue of nuclear missile deployment in the FRG. In 1979, the USA made the decision to station nuclear missiles in Europe. In 1983, the FRG announced that the first Pershing II medium-range nuclear missiles were to be deployed in the FRG. This was met with widespread public opposition with candlelit parades and petitions. The SPD expressed strong opposition to the deployment. However, the Green Party was the main beneficiary of popular opposition. It had previously won seats in state elections in Bremen, and now entered the *Bundestag* in 1983. (The growth of the Green Party was also significant in reducing the electoral base of the SPD.) The following year, in January 1984, enhanced-range missiles were reported in the Soviet press as having been deployed in the GDR. Later, in 1985, the FRG endorsed US President Reagan's '**Star Wars Project**' and the use of West German technology and research to support the

Key term

Star Wars Project
The development of space-based systems to protect the USA from nuclear missile attacks.

development of NATO weapons systems. From 1983, the Green
Party remained a minority but significant force in German
politics. Its success in German government was demonstrated
when **Joschka Fischer** was later appointed Germany's Foreign
Minister in 1998 in Schröeder's Red–Green coalition government.

Conclusion: the FRG's achievements

Overall, the FRG's post-war achievements were considerable.
Within two decades of the FRG's establishment in 1949, it had
established a successful democracy and an extremely powerful
economy. By the 1980s its democracy had also weathered the
challenge from extremists, although not without some curtailment
of democratic freedom. It was beginning to address the burdens
of the past and had also coped with economic crises more
successfully than many other Western states. Furthermore, in spite
of the fluctuations in the wider Cold War international relations,
Ostpolitik improved the FRG's relations with the 'other Germany',
and the Eastern bloc in general. This was achieved simultaneously
with the FRG's maintaining sound relations with the USA and
closer ties with the EEC.

The FRG's economic strength, its political pursuit of the
principles of *Ostpolitik*, and its relations with other powers were to
be significant factors in the unexpected and extremely rapid
chain of events from the summer of 1989 to the autumn of 1990.

**Joschka Fischer
1948–**
Became a Green
Party MP in 1983
and was a popular
and controversial
figure in German
politics, especially
for his previous
active participation
in student politics
and for attacking a
police officer
during a
demonstration in
1973.

Key figure

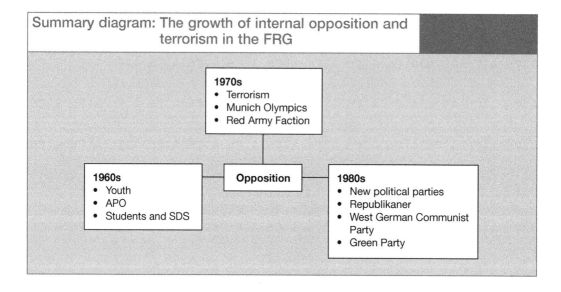

Summary diagram: The growth of internal opposition and terrorism in the FRG

1970s
- Terrorism
- Munich Olympics
- Red Army Faction

1960s
- Youth
- APO
- Students and SDS

Opposition

1980s
- New political parties
- Republikaner
- West German Communist Party
- Green Party

Study Guide: AS Question

In the style of Edexcel

To what extent did relations between East and West Germany change in the 1970s?

Exam tips

The cross-references are intended to take you straight to the material that will help you to answer the question.

The key words to think about when planning your answer to this question are 'relations' and 'change'. In dealing with this question, there is no need to describe at length the actions of Brandt or Ulbricht. A question with the word 'change' in is looking for comparisons: for the ways in which relations became different. 'To what extent' requires you to make an evaluation. To do this you should also identify elements of continuity.

The key change that flowed from Brandt's policy of *Ostpolitik* was a spirit of working to undermine communist control through Eastward-looking *rapprochement*. This replaced Adenauer's policy of resisting communist influence through the strength of Western integration.

The evidence of change in the less strained relations can be shown in:

- the ending of disputes over the GDR's eastern border in 1970 in the Moscow and Warsaw Treaties (page 80)
- improved communications between FRG and West Berlin through the Four-Power Agreement 1971 (page 80)
- the abandonment of the Hallstein Doctrine and GDR's and FRG's mutual recognition in the Basic Treaty paved the way for effective co-operation in a range of areas (pages 70 and 80)
- the FRG gave huge loans to the GDR, increasing the dependence of the GDR on the FRG (page 83).

You could show the following continuities:

- The constitution of the FRG still accorded automatic citizenship to East German citizens and contained the commitment to the formal reuniting of Germany (page 81).
- The FRG did not recognise the GDR as a foreign sovereign state (page 81).
- There were continued escape attempts from the GDR (pages 69–70).
- The propaganda campaigns of the two regimes and systems continued (pages 36–7).

In coming to your overall conclusion you should decide the extent to which *Ostpolitik* fundamentally altered the relationship between the two states in the 1970s.

Study Guide: A2 Question

In the style of AQA

'West German leaders dealt successfully with their domestic problems in the years 1969 to 1989.' Assess the validity of this view.

Exam tips

The cross-references are intended to take you straight to the material that will help you to answer the question.

In order to answer this question you will first need to identify the domestic problems faced by the West German leaders. Look again at Table 2.1 on page 36 and the information on pages 41–51. Before you begin, you would be advised to make a list of the main problems faced by the West German leaders and make some comments on success and failure alongside each one.

You will need to address:

- the fall in economic growth and rising unemployment
- government spending
- the oil crisis
- left-wing opposition and extremism
- youth
- the state of the political parties and political leadership.

In your conclusion you should provide a judgement on the degree to which problems were addressed and you may like to challenge the concept of the FRG as a 'model democracy'.

4

Developments in the GDR Under Honecker 1971–88

POINTS TO CONSIDER

At first Honecker's rule gave grounds for optimism in the GDR. More consumer goods were available and desperately needed housing was being built. The GDR developed its international standing, and its increasing confidence included improving relations with the FRG. However, the increasing links between the GDR and the FRG were problematic for the SED. They reduced some dissent, but also heightened resentment among many ordinary East Germans about some aspects of life in the GDR.

By the 1980s the GDR faced severe economic problems, radical changes in Soviet foreign policy and the growth of reform movements in much of the Eastern bloc. These combined to present clear dilemmas for the SED government.

These issues will be explored through the following key themes:

- The GDR's foreign relations during the 1970s
- Honecker's domestic policies in the 1970s
- The extent of state repression in the GDR
- The declining fortunes of the GDR in the 1980s

Key dates

1972 Basic Treaty between the two Germanys was signed
1974 New constitution redefined the GDR as the 'Republic of Workers' and Peasants' State'
1975 Friendship Treaty between the USSR and the GDR was signed
1985 Gorbachev became leader of the USSR
1987 Honecker became the first leader of the GDR to visit the FRG

1 | The GDR's Foreign Relations During the 1970s

Relations between the two Germanys

Key question
How did relations between the two Germanys develop in the 1970s?

In the 1970s and 1980s Honecker rejected any aim of reuniting Germany. Instead he emphasised a policy of 'demarcation' to stress the differences between East and West Germany and to develop a stronger and clearer sense of the GDR's own unique national identity:

- A new constitution in 1974 redefined the GDR as a distinct state and it officially became the 'Republic of Workers' and Peasants' State'. This emphasised the GDR as the true 'German' state and its justification as the only true German 'anti-fascist' state organised on the basis of class consciousness. The SED promoted itself as the natural successor to Marx and Engels, who, of course, were Germans.
- The East German government portrayed the FRG as too Americanised (which was incidentally a thought which was shared by many West German conservatives) and also claimed the GDR bore no responsibility for the war crimes that had been committed by Nazi Germany.

Key date
New constitution redefined the GDR as the 'Republic of Workers' and Peasants' State': 1974

Honecker's policy of developing a confident, separate GDR identity was demonstrated in daily life in the GDR. German television was renamed GDR television. East German exports were no longer labelled 'Made in Germany' but proudly stated 'Made in the GDR'. However, this separate identity was still undermined by the FRG. Some GDR citizens were annoyed when West German sports commentators sometimes referred to any medals gained by the FRG as won by 'Germans' and any GDR winners as 'from the Soviet zone'. It was not until 1988 that the West German tabloid newspaper *Das Bild* stopped using inverted commas whenever it mentioned the GDR. This use of inverted commas symbolised the newspaper's non-acceptance of East Germany.

Travel and communication between the two Germanys

Key question
How did communication between the FRG and the GDR change?

West German Chancellors from Brandt onwards showed a commitment to improving relations between the two Germanys by continuing the policy of *Ostpolitik*. A very real benefit of this increasing dialogue and co-operation between the Germanys was that West Germans were now able to visit friends and family in the GDR and, although with very severe restrictions, some East Germans were permitted to visit West Germany:

- In 1972 the Basic Treaty between the two Germanys was signed (see pages 80–1 in Chapter 3). This acknowledged each other's independence and 'normalised' relations between them, although it did mean that West Germans now required visas to enter East Berlin rather than the previous daily passes.
- Honecker announced that those East German citizens who had left the GDR illegally before 1972 would no longer face prosecution for 'flight from the republic' if they returned to the GDR to visit friends or relatives.

Key date
Basic Treaty between the two Germanys was signed: 1972

- From 1973 it was no longer illegal for GDR citizens to watch West German television or listen to Western radio stations. This exposure by GDR citizens to West German television and radio was highly significant in continually undermining the East German government's messages and propaganda. It also increased the ambition of GDR citizens to have the right to travel abroad. This was an issue that the other Eastern bloc governments did not have to contend with as their citizens did not have access to Western media in the same language as their own. Access to Western newspapers, however, was tightly controlled and many Western visitors would have newspapers taken from them when crossing the border into East Berlin or into the GDR.
- There were also significant improvements in the postal service and telephone lines between East and West Berlin. It was not until 1970 that there had been any official telephone lines between the two halves of the city.
- A new motorway was constructed from Hamburg to Berlin as part of the plan for the FRG to improve its links with West Berlin. This was, of course, also useful for those travelling within the GDR itself. The FRG funded both its construction and maintenance costs, as it had done with the other two motorways linking the FRG with West Berlin.

From 1972, the official SED government's policy on travel arrangements between the GDR and the FRG rested on the theory that as time passed, family and friendship connections would obviously diminish and, therefore, the East Germans' desire to travel to the West would simply decrease. What this obviously failed to appreciate was that many East Germans simply wanted to be allowed the freedom to travel. The end of travel restrictions was to be one of the major demands in the demonstrations from the summer of 1989 onwards that ultimately led to the opening of the Berlin Wall in November 1989.

Restrictions on travel from the GDR

Travel from the GDR to West Berlin and West Germany remained tightly restricted. Despite being a signatory, the SED refused to comply with the human rights aspects of the 1975 **Helsinki Accords** which were designed to ensure free movement between different countries. Overall, travel to the West was far more restricted from the GDR than from Poland and Hungary. Apart from some business trips, international sports participants, and selected spectators for sports events, it was almost impossible for anyone of working age in the GDR to be issued with the required travel permits to visit the West. East German pensioners were allowed to travel to the FRG, for the cynical reason that if they did not return it reduced the economic burdens on the GDR of a very aged population.

Individuals of working age would sometimes be issued with travel visas to visit family members for 'urgent' reasons, but they had to travel alone; their spouses and children could not

Key question
What travel was allowed West from the GDR?

Key term

Helsinki Accords
A series of agreements signed by 35 European states as well as the USSR and the USA in 1975, aimed at improving international relations.

accompany them. This was obviously intended to serve as emotional pressure to ensure they returned to the GDR. They also knew that, if they failed to return, their families would almost certainly be subjected to extensive *Stasi* surveillance and very possible restrictions on their career and educational opportunities. Honecker also created a new class of citizen in the GDR known as the 'secret-carriers'. These were senior SED government officials, army officers or scientists. The very nature of their occupations meant that they were strictly forbidden to have any contact with Westerners and were not permitted to travel to the West.

Discouragement of Western visitors

The SED was anxious that its citizens were being increasingly exposed to Western influence and media. There had also been alarm in government circles about the high level of popular support that had been displayed for Brandt when he had visited the GDR in 1970 (see page 80). In November 1973, the GDR doubled the amount of currency that Westerners needed to exchange into East German currency when visiting East Berlin. The result was that the numbers from West Berlin visiting East Berlin decreased by more than a third in 1974. There was also a further immediate reaction by the East German government when the FRG announced NATO's deployment of nuclear weapons on West German soil in 1983. Honecker responded with further increases in the amount of hard currency that Western visitors had to exchange into GDR currency to enter East Berlin; this again led to an immediate fall in the number of visitors from the FRG to the GDR. The minimum charge was doubled for extended visits and quadrupled for day passes. Children and pensioners, who had previously been exempt from these financial exchange controls, were now also included. This led to a further decline in the number of visitors.

Relaxations in control of travel and migration

Travel arrangements were slightly relaxed from the mid-1980s onwards. The number of permitted visits also increased. By the late 1980s over a million GDR citizens below retirement age had been granted permission to visit the FRG and, in early 1989, appeal procedures were introduced in the GDR for those who had been refused a passport. However, since this measure was introduced shortly before the opening of the wall, it is impossible to judge what effects it would have had in practice.

Further, prior to the mid-1980s, it is estimated that up to 100,000 GDR citizens had tried to take advantage of the Helsinki Accords and had applied for permission to emigrate, but Honecker's government had not accepted these requests. Those that did apply to emigrate were also often subjected to lengthy interrogations, faced discrimination in education or employment and some were even charged with treason and imprisoned. In 1984, the GDR government allowed 40,000 East German citizens to emigrate to the FRG. A significant proportion of those allowed to emigrate were those seen by the SED as politically unreliable or who were the most active in promoting internal opposition.

The GDR's international relations

Key question
In what ways did the GDR gain greater international recognition?

Western relations

The beginnings of *Ostpolitik* and the Four-Power Agreement led to wider international recognition of the GDR. Both Germanys had applied for, and were accepted as, members of the United Nations in 1973. The GDR now had increasing international status, which included acceptance by the USA. In 1974, in the 25th anniversary celebrations of the founding of the GDR, no references were made to reuniting Germany. Over 90 countries officially recognised the GDR between 1969 and 1974. It was also

---

Profile: Erich Honecker 1912–94

1912	– Born the son of a coal miner in the Saarland
1929	– Joined the German Communist Party (KPD)
1928–30	– Worked as a roofer
1930	– Went to the USSR to study at the International Lenin School
1931	– Returned to Germany
1937	– Sentenced under the Nazis to 10 years' imprisonment for communist activities
1945	– In charge of Free German Youth movement (FDJ)
1958	– Became a full member of the GDR Politburo
1971	– Initiated a power struggle which overthrew Ulbricht and became General Secretary of the SED
1989	– Resigned as General Secretary of the SED
1994	– Died in exile in Chile

Honecker was General Secretary of the GDR from his ousting of Ulbricht in 1971 until his resignation in the autumn of 1989. The period was officially labelled by the SED as 'the further formation of the developed socialist society'. When Honecker first came to power it seemed that the country was making significant advances. The building of the Berlin Wall meant that as there was no longer mass emigration, some real economic progress could be achieved. Honecker wanted to increase the availability of consumer goods and he also prioritised the building of new housing. During his period in office there were significant increases in welfare provision and the GDR was increasingly recognised internationally.

After the reunification of Germany, Honecker went to the USSR but was extradited by the Soviet leader Yeltsin to the newly reunited Germany. He was briefly imprisoned and tried for crimes carried out during the Cold War, especially for ordering GDR border guards to shoot those attempting to cross the Berlin Wall. During his brief court appearance in December 1992 he justified the construction of the Berlin Wall. Honecker was, however, suffering from cancer and so he was released. Honecker and his wife eventually settled in Chile.

in 1974 that the only football match between the GDR and the FRG was played. It was a first round match for the 1974 World Cup with an away win of 1–0 for the GDR. In 1975 the GDR took part in the Helsinki Conference. Its place as an independent sovereign nation was recognised by its participation and its signature to the resulting Helsinki Accords.

Official state visits showed that the GDR's prestige and international standing were clearly increasing. Honecker made his first state visit to a Western state to Austria in 1980; the first NATO state that he visited was Italy in 1985. The GDR leader also made official visits to Belgium, Spain, Sweden and France, and there were visits to the GDR from the leaders of Greece, Austria and Denmark. Honecker enjoyed the opportunities these events gave for press coverage and the increasing international recognition of the GDR. Honecker never succeeded, however, in his aim of being invited on an official state visit to the UK or the USA, but he did make the first visit by an East German leader to the FRG in 1987 (see pages 77–8).

Relations with the USSR and the Eastern bloc

Key question
How did the citizens of the GDR view the USSR and its Eastern bloc allies?

The attitude of many East Germans towards the USSR was very negative, having been determined by their own personal experiences during the Second World War and the immediate post-war period. Many East Germans had been fed the Nazis' anti-Bolshevik propaganda as well as having experienced at first hand the sheer brutality of the Red Army at the end of the Second World War. Despite the heavy air raids that were carried out by the British and USA, many Germans were most bitter about the Soviet role during the war and afterwards. They could not forget their harsh experiences on the **Eastern Front**, the millions of German soldiers who had been held as prisoners of war (some until 1955) and the raping of thousands of Berlin women by Soviet soldiers. They blamed the USSR for the post-war refugee crisis and resented the loss of Germany's eastern territories to Poland. Many also fiercely resented the reparations that had been taken by the USSR in the initial post-war period. It is worth reiterating that the June 1953 uprising in the GDR had been primarily anti-Soviet and only secondarily opposed to Ulbricht and the East German government.

Eastern Front
The scene of military conflict between Germany and the USSR, including much of Eastern Europe, during the Second World War.

Key term

The East German government made considerable efforts to develop a sense of friendship and solidarity between the GDR and the USSR. The SED desperately tried to create among East Germans a feeling of gratitude to the USSR for its significant contribution to the defeat of Nazism. A massive war memorial was erected in Treptower Park in East Berlin in 1949, at a site where nearly 5000 Soviet soldiers had been buried during the Battle for Berlin. The memorial is a statue of a Soviet soldier holding a young German girl he had saved during the Second World War.

However, unlike many West Germans who increasingly saw the British and the USA as their liberators and now their valuable, trusted allies, most East Germans regarded the USSR as an oppressive force which was occupying the GDR. Learning Russian was compulsory in East German schools, but was generally very unpopular. The compulsory study of Marxist–Leninist theory in schools and in higher education did very little to improve attitudes towards the USSR. Although much of the East German population remained fundamentally hostile to the USSR, the GDR government signed an official GDR–Soviet Friendship Treaty in October 1975. This was intended to develop closer links and co-operation between the GDR and the USSR. One of its results was a Society for German–Soviet Friendship, which did become very popular with East German citizens when Gorbachev became Soviet leader; its membership reached over six million in 1988.

As well as a fraught relationship with the USSR, the GDR was on similarly tense terms with other Eastern bloc states. This was also partly a product of the legacies of Nazism and post-war economic difficulties. Despite a shortage of labour in the GDR during the 1970s and a surplus of labour in Poland, both the East German and Polish governments were hesitant to allow a Polish workforce into the GDR until the mid-1970s. Even then, it was under very strict controls and was restricted to the immediate border area of the GDR and Poland. This was mainly due to serious concerns by both the GDR and Polish governments about friction between ordinary Germans and Poles. It was felt that nationalist tensions would override any sense of socialist solidarity. There was also friction when Poles crossed into the GDR to purchase consumer goods that were not available in Poland, which then exacerbated shortages in the GDR. A similar problem over shortages was caused when GDR citizens crossed the border into Czechoslovakia to buy clothes and electrical goods. This led to controls being introduced with Poles having to exchange RM200 when entering East Germany, and Czechoslovakia's imposition of export and customs restrictions on the Czech–GDR border.

Nevertheless, the years 1972–88 saw the sovereignty of the GDR almost universally accepted. The period was marked by the GDR's increasingly confident participation on the international scene and an increase in contact at individual and national level with the 'other Germany'.

Key date

Friendship Treaty between the USSR and the GDR was signed: 1975

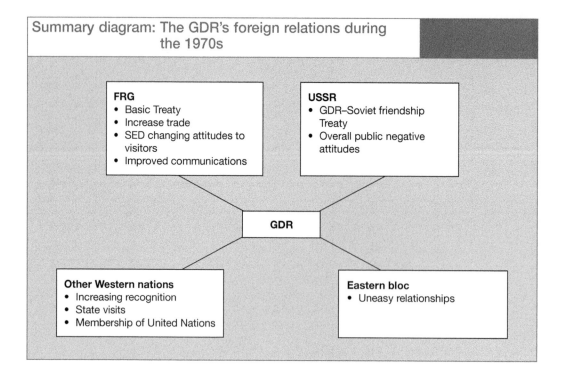

Summary diagram: The GDR's foreign relations during the 1970s

FRG
- Basic Treaty
- Increase trade
- SED changing attitudes to visitors
- Improved communications

USSR
- GDR–Soviet friendship Treaty
- Overall public negative attitudes

GDR

Other Western nations
- Increasing recognition
- State visits
- Membership of United Nations

Eastern bloc
- Uneasy relationships

2 | Honecker's Domestic Policies in the 1970s

The East German economy in the 1970s

Honecker removed much of Ulbricht's 'New Economic System' (see pages 55 and 66–7). Honecker's particular aim was the improvement of the GDR's industrial performance as a vital step towards raising living standards. His message was that the economy and material levels could be improved with greater efficiency and that scientific and technological progress would lead to a 'developed socialist society'. This was the concept of the 'Unity of Social and Economic Policy'. Ultimately, the social aspect of the concept was to prove the undoing of the economic part. Huge expenditure on social reform starved industry of essential investment and contributed to the fundamental economic problems which in turn weakened the GDR's ability to maintain an independent existence. But this emerged in the longer term.

It is arguable that the East German government could justifiably be proud of some aspects of the progress it had made by the mid-1970s. By the 1970s, the GDR claimed to be tenth in the world's top industrial nations having achieved an 'economic miracle' not dissimilar to the one the FRG had experienced a decade earlier. The East German government also stressed that this had been achieved without the GDR having benefited from financial assistance such as the FRG had received with Marshall Aid. It also emphasised that the GDR's economic advances had been gained in spite of the enormous stripping of its resources by the USSR in the immediate post-war period. By 1970, the GDR had overtaken Poland as the USSR's main trading partner.

Key question
In what ways did the GDR's economy improve?

Overall trade was increasing within COMECON and by the early 1970s, the GDR's universities were producing highly skilled graduates in science and technology.

The economic improvements in the GDR led to a shortage of labour in the early 1970s. Similar to the FRG's recruitment of guest workers in the 1950s and 1960s, the GDR now took on workers from other socialist countries. By the mid-1970s there were 60,000 Vietnamese people working in the GDR, as well as others from Mozambique, Angola and Cuba. In addition, students from other socialist states attended East German universities. Many found themselves in very substandard accommodation and faced difficulties integrating with the main population. They later faced significant hostility during the economic downturn from the mid-1980s onwards.

However, the extent of this success was partly due to unique advantages that the GDR had compared to other members of the Eastern bloc. By the 1980s, the FRG was the GDR's second biggest trading partner after the USSR and nearly a third of the GDR's trade was with the FRG. This 'inter-German' trade was not subject to taxes or tariffs and was a considerable economic advantage to both Germanys. The GDR also received large loans from the FRG. This helped it to achieve a very high level of agricultural production, becoming almost self-sufficient; its farming was increasingly efficient and mechanised, especially when compared to neighbouring Poland.

The economic successes of the 1970s were not built on sufficiently secure foundations, as events in the 1980s were to prove. From its beginning, the GDR had suffered from a shortage of raw materials. This was exacerbated by the oil crisis of 1973. This hit all European countries reliant on oil for so much of their energy needs. COMECON states were cushioned to some extent by their access to the USSR's oil, but nothing could protect the GDR from the general increase in world prices which led to a steep increase in the cost of essential imports on which its manufacturing industries depended. As its balance of trade deteriorated sharply in the mid-1970s, Honecker's government turned increasingly to borrowing in order to maintain spending levels. Its determination to protect the concept of the Unity of Social and Economic Policy led to a refusal to attempt to balance its books, to underinvestment in industry, and to the weaknesses which fed into the political arena in the 1980s (see pages 117 and 119–20).

The standard of living in the GDR

The strength of the economy did produce some clear improvements in the standard of living in the 1970s. The minimum wage was raised in 1971. Incomes generally increased and basic food prices were kept purposefully low by the government. There was full employment and in 1976 retirement pensions were increased, although they remained relatively low. By the mid-1970s, East German living standards were the highest in the Eastern bloc and the majority of homes in the GDR had a refrigerator and a television. By the early 1980s, nearly half of all households owned a car. However, there was sometimes a 12-year wait for a new car. Ironically such long waits meant that second-hand Trabant cars could be up to three times more expensive than a brand new one. The GDR had a higher number of televisions, washing machines and telephones per person than in the rest of the Eastern bloc.

However, a major difficulty for the SED was that East German citizens generally compared their own living standards unfavourably with those in the FRG rather than with their socialist neighbours. By the mid-1980s, East German households had the highest rate of telephone ownership (10 per cent) in the Eastern bloc, but there was a huge disparity with the FRG which had a nearly 100 per cent ownership. Consumer goods that were becoming increasingly available in the West during the 1980s, such as video recorders and microwaves, were simply not available in the GDR. Other goods, such as clothing, were often of a much inferior quality.

A comparison of two ordinary lives in the GDR and the FRG

How different were lives in this divided Germany at the beginning of the 1970s? It is easy to assume that living standards were much higher in the FRG than in GDR. The figures in Box 4.1 are taken from H.W. Schwarze's *The GDR Today*, published in 1970. Schwarze was a well-respected West German journalist and authority on the GDR. What would you deduce from the figures shown?

Box 4.1: Comparing two ordinary lives in the GDR and the FRG (all currency in DM to allow meaningful comparison)

Gerda, a 27-year-old secretary in the GDR earns 500 marks a month	Gerda, a 27-year-old secretary in the FRG earns 900 marks a month
Monthly costs: • Rent for a one-bed flat: 44 marks (no heating costs) • Meals at work: 30 marks • All other bills, including food: 250 marks	Monthly costs: • Rent for one-bed flat: 250 marks • Meals at work: 50 marks • All other bills, including food and heating: 400 marks
Holiday: every three or four years to East German coast	Holiday: one foreign holiday every two years
Will never have a car	Runs an old car

Economic inequalities within the GDR

In spite of the declared socialism of its political leaders, there were economic inequalities among those living in the GDR. There was a chain of Intershops in the GDR which had first been introduced in 1962 with the main purpose of attracting Western currency. These were mainly situated within the GDR on the motorways to and from West Berlin and the FRG, at crossing

Key question
What accounted for economic inequalities in the GDR?

points and at major railway stations and airports. These shops sold Western goods but only accepted Western currency, which was illegal for GDR citizens to possess until 1974. This meant that these goods were available only to those in the GDR who had personal contacts in the West from whom they could obtain Western currency. The Intershops were also frequently staffed by IMs working for the *Stasi* and the taking of photographs of these stores was strictly banned.

The existence of Intershops clearly demonstrated the dilemmas that the East German government faced and Honecker himself was against their existence. However, other members of the Politburo argued that they served as a useful means to reduce public resentment over the shortage of quality consumer goods within the GDR; by 1980 around 400 such shops existed. Unfortunately for the East German government, they also highlighted the superior range and quality of goods available in the FRG and so reinforced resentment as well as creating economic inequalities. In addition, there were chains of Exquisit and Delikat shops which stocked imported goods from the West which did take East German currency, but their prices were simply far too high for the majority of East German citizens.

Other economic inequalities also revealed the SED's hypocrisy. It made bold statements of its commitment to developing a socialist society while leading government figures had access to goods and services denied to the ordinary public. Wandlitz, just north of Berlin, was the home after 1960 for SED leaders and members of the Politburo. Local people nicknamed it Volvograd because of the number of Swedish-built Volvo cars there. The SED justified the town's existence on security grounds. Those who lived there led very isolated lives away from the general public. It included shopping, health and sports facilities which were of a considerably higher standard than those that were available to the general public. It also included a nuclear bunker, which was completed in 1983 and which was the most advanced within the Eastern bloc, with nearly 200 rooms and accommodation for up to 400 people. Similarly, the island of Vilm on the GDR's Baltic coast had been completely sealed off to the general public in 1959 and was used as an exclusive holiday resort for senior government members. As well as revealing the government's double standards, such facilities also meant that many of the ruling élite had little real understanding of the daily lives of most East German citizens.

Social issues in the GDR
The role of women in the GDR

Key question
How women-friendly were economic policies in the GDR?

Many policies pursued by the East German government were determined by GDR's demography. The overall population of the GDR actually fell from its establishment in 1949 at over 18 million to fewer than 17 million by 1989. This was primarily the result of the high numbers emigrating from the GDR before the building of the wall in 1961. By the 1970s, the GDR was faced with an ageing population with only just over half of the GDR population of working age. This severely hampered economic progress as well as being a financial burden on the state.

One particular consequence of this was that the government prioritised the employment of as many women as possible. In 1972 a new and extended series of welfare provisions were introduced to encourage women to have more children. These included higher maternity benefits and increased birth allowances for each child. These were further increased in both 1976 and 1984, making maternity leave the most generous in the world, with women entitled to a full year's maternity leave, and a year and a half for a third child or more. There was also an entitlement to one day a month off work for household duties. There was also extensive state provision for pre-school care and after-school activities. Universities and colleges also had to provide arrangements for student mothers, with a flexible system of examinations if necessary.

By the late 1980s, at over 90 per cent, the GDR had one of the highest proportions of women in paid employment in the world. There were determined efforts to encourage women to pursue careers in science and technology. However, women still tended to be disproportionately employed in lower-skilled occupations and although by the late 1970s women made up half of all doctors, dentists and teachers, they seldom occupied senior positions. Very few women were represented in the government. The only woman to reach high office in politics was Honecker's own wife, Margot Honecker (nicknamed the 'purple dragon' by East Germans because of her hairstyle), who was GDR Education Minister from 1963 to 1989. But even this position did not give her membership of the policy-making Politburo.

Housing in the GDR

Rents were purposefully kept extremely low. The average rent in the GDR was around five per cent of income (compared to an average of 30 per cent in the FRG). The vast majority of housing in the GDR was poor by Western standards. When Honecker became leader, much of the GDR's housing was old and had been built in the late nineteenth and early twentieth centuries. Honecker recognised the need to reduce the serious housing shortage (which was also partly a consequence of the very high divorce rate in the GDR) and claimed that it would be solved by 1990. In 1971, the SED announced an ambitious building programme which aimed to create four million new homes by 1989. Figures released after the reuniting of Germany showed that less than two million new homes had been built between 1971 and 1988; a much lower number than was officially claimed at the time by the SED.

Key question
How was housing in the GDR improved under Honecker?

A statue of Lenin in East Berlin with high-rise *Plattenbauen* behind.

The building programme led to the development of large-scale housing estates such as Marzahn and Hellersdorf on the outskirts of East Berlin, and new towns such as Halle-Neustadt. The vast majority of these desperately needed new residential buildings were ***Plattenbauen***, cheaply and quickly constructed tower blocks or rows of houses in large areas on the outskirts of many major towns and cities. In their time they were highly sought after although since the reuniting of Germany, many have been left unoccupied due to a combination of the decreasing population in many parts of the former GDR and the availability of more modern forms of housing.

Key term

Plattenbauen
Buildings made
from concrete slabs.

The Protestant Church in the GDR

Key question
What role did the
Protestant Church
play in the GDR?

Honecker and the SED had also began to show more tolerance and general acceptance of the Protestant Church than during Ulbricht's government, or in fact most other Eastern bloc states, which generally followed repressive policies towards religion. Relations between church and state had basically been hostile since the foundation of the GDR until the beginnings of a tentative and cautious relationship between the government and the church was written into the new GDR constitution in 1968. A new agreement was made in March 1978 when the first meeting for 20 years between state and church took place. The Protestant Church acknowledged its need to work within the socialist society. In return its role within the state increased. After this, the SED permitted religious television broadcasts and chaplains were allowed to make prison visits.

The church played a significant role in health and education. The Protestant Church in the GDR ran over 50 hospitals and a large number of old people's homes. It also received financial support from church groups in the FRG. The church also provided a useful tool for the SED in supporting those who were officially denounced by the state as hostile to 'actually existing socialism'. These included alcoholics (alcoholism was a major problem in the GDR), drug addicts (whose numbers were very low compared to the FRG) and homosexuals.

As part of a limited and cautious liberalisation of some aspects of policy following the Helsinki Accords, the 1978 March Agreement allowed open discussion of political issues to take place under the umbrella of the church and as part of a religious meeting. The rationale for this relaxation appears to have been the belief that expression of discontent would prevent its build-up and that the priests, in return for the freedom of discussion, could be relied on to keep it under control. After the reunification of Germany, it was also revealed that some leading members of the church had *Stasi* connections. Nonetheless, church attendance in the GDR represented around a third of the population, and what began as a measure to control or prevent dissent increasingly became a channel for it. The Protestant Church became a focal point for opposition to the government during the 1980s. It also played a significant role in the 1989 demonstrations (see Chapter 5, pages 132–3).

Summary diagram: Honecker's domestic policies in the 1970s

Achievements	Limitations
• Rising living standards • Church–State agreement • Trade • *Plattenbauen* • Women's employment	• Disparity with FRG • Economic inequality within GDR • Women under-represented in key occupations • Underlying economic weakness

3 | The Extent of State Repression in the GDR

The work of the *Stasi*

Key question
How extensive was
surveillance by the
Stasi in the GDR?

The East German government relied on state intimidation and surveillance of its own people with the *Stasi*, its extensive state security police. At its height in the mid-1970s the *Stasi* employed 180,000 full-time staff. To these can be added the IM collaborators. There are estimates that at any time, around 20 per cent of the GDR population were working for the *Stasi*. The size of the *Stasi*, which was far greater than the state security apparatus in the other neighbouring Eastern bloc states, was justified by the SED on the grounds that their Warsaw Pact allies did not have to contend with a neighbouring state such as the FRG or the unique issues that arose from a divided Berlin.

After 1989 it emerged that state surveillance had been much more widespread than many had believed. *Stasi* files showed that around three-quarters of the adult population had been under surveillance at some point in their lives from the vast network of informers. Since the fall of the Berlin Wall, some individuals have had access to their files. These dossiers often included a vast amount of detailed information, ranging from what time people got up, their route to work, what they bought in shops, and when they normally turned their lights off. There was 180 km of shelving for the documents. Some 90,000 letters had been opened daily and telephone lines had often been tapped. Many people prudently added a few lines in personal letters expressing support for the government. In fact, it would seem that the *Stasi* collected far more information than it could possibly deal with.

The *Stasi* used various methods to track down opponents to the government. Even the smells of individuals were collected and stored. Sometimes *Stasi* officers broke into people's homes and took items of clothing to collect an individual's smell, should the future need arise for tracker dogs to follow their scent. They even used cameras hidden in cigarette boxes and ties. Hotel receptionists were often employed as IMs. There are estimates that at any one time, a quarter of the staff at the Humboldt University (East Berlin's main university) had connections with the *Stasi*.

Hohenschönhausen

Key question
Why was
Hohenschönhausen
so infamous?

Between 1951 and 1989 the *Stasi* used Hohenschönhausen, in the eastern suburbs of East Berlin, as a prison for those awaiting sentence. Many people were held as political prisoners, and it was infamous for its regime of physical and psychological torture. The prison was originally used in the immediate post-war period by the Soviets as Special Camp Number 3. It was taken over by the East German *Stasi* in 1951 and was used to detain many after the June 1953 uprising was well as Jehovah's Witnesses and those found guilty of 'flight from the republic'.

Much of the area around the prison was a restricted zone with very limited access. It was deliberate policy that the prisoners had no idea of their whereabouts. To disorientate them after their arrest, the prisoners were blindfolded and driven around in circles in a car that stopped and started frequently. The same would happen if they were later released. Interestingly, by 1989, even before the opening of the Berlin Wall, prison staff just released prisoners at the gate rather than taking them through the long disorientation process. Perhaps this was a sign that many of the SED and *Stasi* were well aware that the GDR's days were numbered.

Increased repression from the mid-1970s

The mid-1970s onwards was a period of increased repression that coincided with the economic crisis. The East German government was increasingly aware that its control was slipping. Prominent writers and critics of the government were targeted, despite the government having signed the Helsinki Accords in 1975.

Key question
How were some well-known writers treated by the East German government?

In 1976 for example, a popular East German singer, Wolf Biermann, had been granted a travel visa for a concert tour in the FRG. He was part of a group of other East German writers and artists who had been campaigning for more freedom within the GDR. However, on his return, his East German citizenship was taken away. The government claimed that during the tour while in Cologne, FRG, he had spoken against the GDR. He was not allowed back into the GDR, even though he had a wife and children there. There is evidence to suggest that the GDR had organised this before he had actually left the country.

In an open letter, a group of well-known East German authors and artists, including Christa Wolf and Stefan Heym, criticised the government's actions. Heym had also written an account of the June 1953 uprising, which had been banned and had led Honecker to consider charging him with treason. Rudolf Bahro was a critic of the government and was sentenced to eight years' imprisonment for writing a book published in the FRG describing the problems of the GDR. He was released after a year following protest from the West. In December 1975 many Western journalists were expelled from the GDR and in April 1979 the East German government imposed severe restrictions on all foreign journalists, who now needed official government permission before holding any interviews.

4 | The Key Debate

What was the extent of state repression in the GDR?

The main debates on this period focus on the extent to which the SED controlled and penetrated people's lives, and whether there was genuine support for socialism from East German citizens or whether it was simply imposed on a population that was never committed to the ideology.

The standard Cold War image of the GDR is of a totalitarian state that relied on ruthless suppression and an extensive secret police network to maintain control. It portrays the East German population as essentially imprisoned by the heavily guarded

Berlin Wall and the 'inner-German border'. The GDR was simply subservient to, and controlled by the USSR. However, since the end of the Cold War, historians have had access to more archives and individual accounts of personal histories. Gradually, much more diverse interpretations have emerged which see the GDR in more complex terms than that of the simple Cold War portrayal.

Mary Fulbrook argues that many GDR citizens were able to lead completely normal lives and did not come into contact with state surveillance. This argument also maintains that there was also some real public approval for the government's policies on issues such as housing and on careers for women. She notes that the East German dictatorship, with its numerous party functionaries, *Stasi* informers and honorary office holders, actually had many citizens who were active participants and supporters of the government's socialist aims. However, Fulbrook also argues that this popular support for the regime was undermined by resentment and frustrations regarding the shortage of goods, the limited career opportunities and restrictions on travel.

Andrew Port argues that the years 1953–89 were remarkably stable given that many East Germans were not loyal to the state and that many GDR citizens complained about working conditions, housing and the shortage of consumer goods. However, local SED groups were anxious to avoid confrontation and made what concessions they could. The SED also cleverly exploited gender, age, educational and income differences to reduce the threat of a united opposition forming against the government.

The concept of the niche society and the degree of popular support for the GDR

Key term

Niche society
People showing loyalty towards the state and socialism in public, while developing personal fulfilment and interests within close-knit family and friendship groups.

The concept of the **niche society** was first used by Günter Gaus, the FRG's main representative in the GDR. Fulbrook summarises his view as 'East Germans came to terms with the pressures and demands of the regime by leading a double life of outward conformity combined with private authenticity'. This concept has been used to explain the GDR's stability, in that it did not depend simply on control and coercion of the people by the state. The population developed a means of coming to terms with life under the regime. The majority of ordinary East Germans displayed support for the country in public, and then retreated into their own private lives, away from the pressures of conformity, where they could then express their opinions more openly and frankly among those whom they trusted.

It is a difficult for historians to assess the actual extent to which a population living under a dictatorship does genuinely support its government. The notion of a niche society has not only been used to study the GDR, it has been used to describe ordinary people's lives in other parts of the Eastern bloc during the post-war period, and also those who had lived under the Nazi dictatorship.

With specific reference to the GDR the main arguments for and against the amount of support for the regime are summarised in Box 4.2.

Box 4.2: A summary of the two main viewpoints regarding the extent of support for the GDR

There was genuine support for and loyalty to the GDR and the goals of socialism from a significant number of the population	There was a general dissatisfaction with the GDR and the need for personal retreat to a 'niche'
1. There was relative satisfaction for life in the GDR. The country was economically successful compared to the rest of the Eastern bloc. The GDR's sporting achievements developed a sense of national pride.	1. Most East Germans compared their standard of living with the FRG unfavourably and were frustrated by the lack of consumer goods and restrictions on travel.
2. Following the construction of the Berlin Wall and the increasing sense of Germany's permanent division, many were actually determined to work towards improvements in the GDR.	2. There were examples of opposition, such as the June 1953 uprising and objections to the building of the Berlin Wall, and there was clearly increasing discontent by the 1980s. An assassination attempt in 1982 on Honecker was immediately hushed up. The lack of opposition was mainly due to extensive *Stasi* surveillance.
3. In 1988, mass organisations such as the Democratic Women's Association of Germany had 1.5 million members and the Free German Youth had 2.5 million members, even though membership was not compulsory. Such groups fostered belief in the state.	3. Many joined the mass organisations, not out of loyalty to the state, but to ensure they did not jeopardise their educational and employment opportunities. The mass organisations were used by the SED to control how individuals spent their leisure time. The mass public parades and cheering on days such as May Day, the GDR's anniversary, the anniversary of the deaths of Rosa Luxemburg and Karl Liebknecht, and the FDJ marches did not indicate approval and support for the government.
4. There were no major protests after the June 1953 uprising until the summer of 1989. This was in contrast to Hungary, Czechoslovakia and Poland where challenges to the government needed Soviet intervention to suppress them.	4. The high suicide rate in the GDR led Ulbricht to put a ban on the publication of the figures in 1963, which remained in force for the rest of the GDR's history.
5. The initial protests in 1989 were more focused on reform within the GDR and not on reunification with the FRG.	5. The protests in 1989 soon moved towards support for German reunification.

Some key books in the debate

M. Fulbrook, *The People's State: East German Society from Hitler to Honecker* (Yale, 2005)

M. Fulbrook, *Anatomy of a Dictatorship* (Oxford, 1995)

A. Port, *Conflict and Stability in the GDR* (Cambridge, 2007)

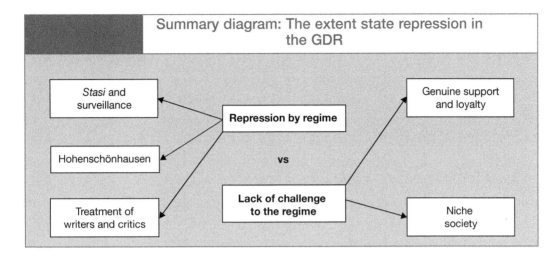

Summary diagram: The extent state repression in the GDR

5 | The Declining Fortunes of the GDR in the 1980s

Key question
How did economic problems affect the GDR in the 1980s?

Table 4.1:
Percentage of gross national product spending on defence in 1978

Bulgaria	2.5
Czechoslovakia	3.8
GDR	5.8
Hungary	2.4
Poland	3.0
Romania	1.7

The East German economy in the 1980s

The economic downturn that followed the oil crisis of the mid-1970s (see page 107) produced clear signs of stagnation in the GDR. This was largely, but not entirely a result of policies that Honecker had followed. To increase productivity and industrial modernisation, Honecker had borrowed heavily, and from the mid-1970s the GDR had accumulated large debts. It was also exacerbated by the high expenditure on defence (Table 4.1). Overall, attempts to boost trade were unsuccessful. The quality of consumer goods was often inferior, leading to a lack of competitiveness, and production costs were increasing because of the rising costs of essential imports needed by manufacturing industries. Such a situation led the historians, Kuhrt, Buck and Holzweissig, to describe the GDR's economy by the mid-1980s as 'moribund'.

By the mid-1980s, both industrial growth and incomes were falling. The SED, however, deliberately manipulated the official government statistics to give a misleading impression of the state of the GDR's economy. Honecker then initiated a number of measures:

- Increased East German exports by taking goods (such as furniture) out of the GDR domestic market. This led to shortages for East German consumers. Many East Germans did accumulate large savings accounts in the 1980s, but this was because there was often simply nothing available for them to spend their money on.
- Arranged credit from the FRG: the GDR borrowed large sums. There was for example, in 1983, at the height of the Cold War, a credit payment of DM1 billion from the FRG to the GDR. Table 4.2 shows the increasing levels of foreign debt in the GDR and Table 4.3 shows the deficit in the GDR's trade with the FRG by the mid-1980s.

- Reduced domestic spending. This obviously affected the quality of life in the GDR. Public buildings, transport and roads deteriorated.
- Attempted to build the economy by exchanging East German military expertise with countries such as Algeria, Angola, Ethiopia, Mozambique, Syria and Zimbabwe in return for raw materials.
- Sold an average of approximately 1500 political prisoners each year to the FRG between 1980 and 1985.

Table 4.2: Foreign debt of the GDR 1970–87 (in DM billions)

Year	Debt
1970	2.2
1975	11.0
1980	25.3
1985	30.0
1987	34.7

Table 4.3: GDR trade with the FRG 1981–5 (in DM millions)

Year	GDR to FRG	FRG to GDR	GDR trade surplus/deficit
1981	6100	5800	300
1983	6800	7000	−200
1985	7600	7900	−300

Diverging societies? A comparison of the economies and standards of living of the GDR and FRG

Comparisons of the 1980s with the immediate post-war period reveal that the FRG became industrialised and urbanised to a much greater degree than the GDR. The West also outpaced the East in population growth (Table 4.4). There were also differences in pattern of employment in the 1980s which reflected the nature and priorities of the two different economic systems: one capitalist and the other socialist. The West had a higher proportion of employees in service industries, the East a higher proportion of employees in state employment (Table 4.6). The key difference which caused most discontent in the GDR was the relative lack of consumer choice in the East (Table 4.7), except for that granted to the privileged few (see pages 108–9). However, the most striking difference revealed by Table 4.4 below, is the relatively slow rate of economic change in the East. Nevertheless, Table 4.5 provides evidence of the success of the two economies as leaders within their respective blocs, while confirming the economic lead of the FRG over the GDR.

Key question
How different were the economies and societies of the two Germanys by the late 1980s?

Table 4.4: Changes in population and its distribution

	Western Germany 1939	FRG 1980	Eastern Germany 1939	GDR 1980
Population	43 million	62 million	17 million	17 million

	Western Germany 1950	FRG 1980	Eastern Germany 1950	GDR 1980
Percentage living in communities of <2000 people	29	24	29	6
Percentage living in communities of <10,000 people	48	74	48	57
Percentage living in communities of 10,000–100,000 people	21	40	27	31

Table 4.5: Gross national product per head 1979 (US dollars)

FRG	11,730	GDR	6,430
France	9,940	USSR	4,110
Austria	8,620	Poland	3,830
UK	6,340	Yugoslavia	1,900
Italy	5,240		

Table 4.6: Employment patterns in 1983

Occupations	FRG (%)	GDR (%)
Agriculture and forestry	6	11
Trade	13	10
Service sector	16	7
State, education and health	15	18

Table 4.7: A comparison of the percentage ownership of key consumer goods. The figures are for a four-person middle-income family in East and West Germany

Consumer goods	FRG (%)	GDR (%)
Washing machine and fridge	99	99
Black-and-white television	98	94
Colour television	96	52
Car	97	52
Telephone	98	9

As has been shown (see page 108), simple comparisons of goods or incomes do not tell the whole story. Incomes and standards of living in the West were undoubtedly higher, but citizens of the East had an adequate lifestyle, and a greater level of security. High state spending on health and social welfare, generous maternity benefits, comprehensive child-care provision, subsidised food and housing, and adequate retirement pensions: these combined to give the citizens of the GDR security from hunger, want, homelessness or unemployment. All adults of working age had a job, although it might not always have been the job they wanted, or one appropriate to their aptitude and skills. The relative success of welfare provision compared to the GDR's Eastern bloc neighbours is indicated by the infant mortality figures in Table 4.8.

Table 4.8: Infant mortality rates in the Eastern bloc per 1000 live births

	1948	1968
Bulgaria	118	87
Czechoslovakia	84	22
GDR	89	20
Hungary	94	36
Poland	111	33
Romania	143	59

Fulbrook uses such social and economic comparisons to argue that this provision of a 'modest minimum' standard of living had political implications. It meant that there was no revolutionary groundswell to support the dissenting voice of a few intellectuals. She observes 'East Germans were not, before 1989, prepared to rise in a clearly hopeless revolt just because the choice in their fruit and vegetable shops was between cabbages and more cabbages, while the West Germans ate peaches, oranges and grapes.' However, when there appeared to be a greater prospect of revolution in the late 1980s (see pages 121–2), the level of consumer dissatisfaction with this drabness and lack of choice played its part in the chain of events that unfolded.

International relations

Although the policies of the superpowers inevitably influenced the two Germanys in their position as frontline members of opposing blocs, they maintained their unique version of a German *détente* during periods of rising international tension. The late 1970s and early 1980s witnessed increased Cold War tension between the USSR and the USA. In 1979, the USSR invaded Afghanistan and in November the following year Ronald Reagan was elected President of the USA. He soon increased US military spending. Chancellor Schmidt made a hugely symbolic visit to the GDR in 1981 as if to prove to the world that the two Germanys were still pursuing their own policies in the spirit of *détente*, but international Cold War tensions did have an impact. In 1984, both the USA and USSR deployed nuclear missiles in their respective Germanys. A visit which had been scheduled from Honecker to the FRG was cancelled under pressure from Moscow; it eventually took place in 1987.

Key question
Did Cold War tensions affect relations between the two Germanys?

Honecker was the first leader of the GDR to visit the FRG: 1987

Key date

State visit by Erich Honecker (right) to the FRG with Helmut Kohl (left) in September 1987.

Key question
What effect did Gorbachev's reforms have on the GDR?

Gorbachev's reforms in the USSR and their impact on the GDR

Gorbachev's reforms

Soon after becoming leader of the USSR in 1985, Mikhail Gorbachev initiated a programme of reforms, known as *glasnost* and *perestroika*. *Perestroika* included radical economic changes, such as the introduction of private enterprise. *Glasnost* included:

Key date
Gorbachev became leader of the USSR: 1985

- freedom of speech
- free elections
- inclusion of non-communists in government.

These fundamental changes had an impact on the Eastern bloc states.

Changes in the USSR's relationship with the Eastern bloc

For Gorbachev's policies to have any chance of success, Soviet military spending had to be reduced to enable the USSR's weak economy to develop. It was soon clear that the USSR now regarded the Eastern bloc as a severe drain on its resources. There were nearly half a million Soviet troops stationed in the GDR – twice the size of the GDR's own national army. Gorbachev reduced the USSR's deployment of troops in the GDR to fewer than 200,000. To decrease military spending even further, the USSR and NATO agreed in 1987 on the withdrawal of medium-range nuclear missiles from both their respective allies in Europe. By 1988, at a Warsaw Pact meeting, the Soviet Foreign Minister made it clear that the time had now come to end the USSR's commitment to the **Brezhnev Doctrine**. From now on the USSR would not intervene with its armed forces to assist Eastern bloc governments faced with internal dissent.

Key term
Brezhnev Doctrine
The USSR claimed the right to intervene in Eastern bloc states to maintain the unity of the Warsaw Pact.

Changes in the USSR's relations with the FRG

Of further alarm for the GDR was the sudden improvement in relations between the USSR and the FRG. The West German President, Weizsaecker, had made a state visit to Moscow in 1987, which was followed by a Soviet return visit to Bonn. In the autumn of 1988 Kohl visited Gorbachev with a reciprocal visit the following year. Clearly, this rapid improvement in relations between the FRG and the USSR was a destabilising development for the East German government, as David Childs observes: 'this personal rapport between Kohl and Gorbachev could only worry SED leaders'.

Key question
What effect did reform movements in other Eastern bloc states have on the GDR?

The beginnings of reform movements in other parts of the Eastern bloc

The impact of the change in Soviet policy became clear almost immediately. Gorbachev's policies led to the emergence of reform movements in other Eastern bloc states, especially in Poland where the Solidarity movement in 1980 began campaigning against the Polish government. There was also increasing opposition in Czechoslovakia. These movements were demanding even more radical reforms than those beginning to take place in the USSR. The East German government attempted to portray these movements as the result of incitement from the Western powers, but this did not prevent the development of similar demands within the GDR. The SED tried to reduce the growing resentment by claiming that the GDR was in fact ahead of the USSR and was therefore not in need of reform. It re-emphasised the economic progress of the GDR compared to the other Eastern bloc states, the existence of other political parties, and the amount of private enterprise which was allowed. However, Gorbachev's foreign policy changes and domestic reforms encouraged those arguing for reform in the GDR to become more confident. There was increasing resentment and frustration at Honecker's resistance to reform.

Dilemmas for the East German government

Gorbachev's reforms presented Honecker's government with a clear dilemma. If the SED started to undertake reforms and begin to retreat from socialist principles, it would take away the very reason for the GDR's existence. It would be extremely hard, if not impossible, to justify a separate German nation, since the political and economic systems of the two Germanys would essentially become identical. Honecker's position steadily weakened and, as Childs observes, 'like his predecessors, the real threat [to Honecker] came from Moscow'.

This meant that supporters of the regime, who had always argued that the GDR needed to insulate itself from the West, now felt that they had to insulate it from developments in the USSR. This created a division within the SED between those who argued that there was a 'GDR way of doing things' and a need to distance itself from the reforms being undertaken in the USSR, and those who were increasingly frustrated at Honecker's hard line and refusal to reform along lines similar to Gorbachev's.

The increase in repression was evident in the harsh treatment during a demonstration in East Berlin in January 1988 on the official anniversary of the deaths of **Rosa Luxemburg** and **Karl Liebknecht**. The demonstrators carried banners quoting Luxemburg's own words, 'Freedom is the freedom to think differently', but there were nearly 100 arrests.

As part of a policy of trying to detach the GDR from the influence on the USSR, Soviet newspapers, films and magazines were censored by the government. For example, an East German teacher was arrested in 1988 after a Russian lesson when a student reported him to the *Stasi* for using an article in ***Pravda*** which criticised Honecker. In November 1988 the GDR banned the Soviet magazine *Sputnik* in East Germany by claiming that it gave a distorted view of history. Five Soviet films were banned from a film festival in East Berlin. The GDR press also ran an anti-Soviet propaganda campaign reporting on alcoholism, homelessness and food shortages in the USSR.

Key question
What particular problems did Gorbachev's reforms create for the East German government?

Key figures

Rosa Luxemburg (1871–1919) and **Karl Liebknecht (1871–1919)**
Leading communists in Germany after the First World War. They were murdered in 1919 and achieved iconic status in the history of German communism.

Key term

Pravda
The official government newspaper in the USSR.

Even so, in spite of growing questioning of the regime, neither the two German governments, nor the superpowers could have foreseen the rapid chain of events that were to develop from the summer of 1989 onwards.

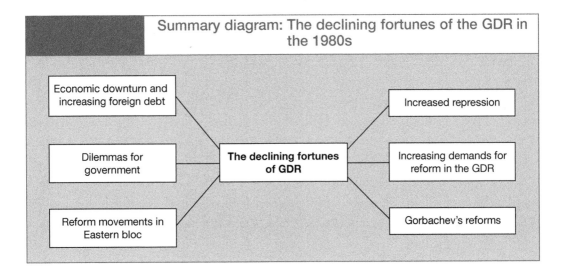

Summary diagram: The declining fortunes of the GDR in the 1980s

Study Guide: AS Question

In the style of Edexcel

How accurate is it to say that the economic achievements of the GDR were limited?

Exam tips

The cross-references are intended to take you straight to the material that will help you to answer the question.

This question also requires you to draw on material in Chapters 1, 2 and 4. In planning your answer, you should gather evidence of economic achievement and also evidence which shows the limitations or inadequacies of what was achieved. You should also make clear the criteria you are applying to make your judgements. One essential element of the answer will be to show what was achieved in relation to the difficulties the GDR faced at the beginning. Be careful, too, not simply to compare the GDR with its successful neighbour, the FRG, but also to consider the GDR's achievement in relation to other members of the Eastern bloc.

Evidence of achievements can be seen in relation to:

- Remarkable progress in the light of the post-war dislocation and extent of Soviet asset stripping for reparations (pages 11, 36, 106–8).
- Success in agricultural production after the initial problems caused by collectivisation (page 52).
- Growing economic strength enabled extensive welfare provision to be introduced (page 119).
- The GDR's economic performance had outstripped that of other members of the Eastern bloc by the mid-1980s (page 106).

The following are evidence of the limitations:

- The persistent lack of a range of consumer goods (pages 117–18).
- Production of goods of inferior quality reduced the GDR's competiveness in world markets (pages 117–18).
- Foreign debts levels were high by the mid-1980s (pages 107 and 117).
- Economic performance was limited in comparison to that of the FRG (pages 108 and 118–19).

Your conclusion will depend on what weight you give to these competing considerations. As long as your criteria for your judgements are clear and well justified on the basis of the evidence, you will gain high marks.

Study Guide: A2 Question

In the style of AQA

How far is it true to say that most East Germans were satisfied with life in the GDR in the 1970s?

Exam tips

The cross-references are intended to take you straight to the material that will help you to answer the question.

In order to answer this question you will need to re-read pages 101–2 that explain restrictions on travel as well as the sections on Honecker's domestic policies and state repression on pages 106–14. This question is effectively focusing on the concept of the niche society (pages 114–15), and Box 4.2 on page 116 should help form a framework for your essay.

You will need to consider the position of different groups, e.g. workers, the professional classes, women and youth, and you could evaluate the importance of:

- state welfare provision, including health, education and social security
- housing
- employment opportunities
- leisure activities
- propaganda and pride in achievements
- repression and indoctrination, including the activities of the *Stasi*
- restrictions on travel
- standard of living and economic inequalities.

You might also comment on the difficulty of assessing what people actually felt in this tightly controlled communist society and although you are likely to comment on the absence of major protest in this period, you would need to balance this against the increase in repression from the mid-1970s.

5 The Reuniting of Germany 1989–91

POINTS TO CONSIDER

Between 1989 and 1990 a rapid chain of events led first to the opening of the Berlin Wall and then to the reuniting of Germany: events which surprised and amazed many throughout the world. How significant to this process were the protest movements inside the GDR and the reforms in the USSR and other Eastern European states? It must not be assumed that the opening of the Berlin Wall in November 1989 would necessarily lead to the end of the GDR as a separate state. Could the GDR have reformed and how significant was Kohl's role as the 'reunification Chancellor?' What was the significance of the responses of the Western Allies and the USSR to the sudden opening of the wall and to the reuniting of Germany?

These issues will be examined through the following key themes:

- The increasing problems of the GDR in the summer of 1989
- The events leading up to the opening of the Berlin Wall
- November 1989: the opening of the Berlin Wall and its immediate impact
- The disintegration of the GDR
- The process of reuniting the GDR and the FRG
- The role of Chancellor Kohl in the reuniting of Germany

Key dates

1989	May 2	Reforming Hungarian government opened its border with Austria
	May 7	Opposition groups in the GDR monitored local election results
	October 6	Gorbachev visited East Berlin for the GDR's 40th anniversary celebrations
	October 18	Honecker resigned and was replaced by Krenz as General Secretary of the SED
	November 6	Monday demonstrators in Leipzig chanted 'Germany – One Fatherland'

	November 9	Unrestricted travel from the GDR to the FRG announced and parts of the Berlin Wall opened
	November 28	Kohl announced his 'Ten-Point Plan'
	December 1	Constitutional change in GDR ended supreme role of the SED
1990	March 18	Free elections to the GDR parliament held
	July 1	Currency union between the FRG and the GDR
	July 16	USSR agreed to reunited Germany being part of NATO
	September 12	Final Two-plus-Four Treaty signed in Moscow
	October 3	GDR was abolished and its territory formally reunited with the FRG
	December 2	First post-war all-German election returned Kohl as Chancellor
1991	November	Final dismantling of the Berlin Wall

1 | The Increasing Problems of the GDR in the Summer of 1989

In January 1989 Honecker proclaimed confidently that the Berlin Wall would stand for another 100 years. However, as we have seen in Chapter 4, the USSR's radical changes in foreign policy, the GDR's dire economic situation and the beginnings of political and economic reforms in other Eastern bloc states were all severe enough problems in themselves to threaten the GDR's stability. They presented major challenges for the East German government. However, a further problem of mass emigration from the GDR began in the summer of 1989 as thousands of East Germans took the opportunity to 'escape' through the East German border with Czechoslovakia into Hungary and through Hungary's newly opened border to Austria and then to the FRG.

The period 1989–90 was a story of spiralling decline in the authority of the GDR government. Fulbrook has stated that in the summer of 1989, 'external changes were sufficiently momentous to generate a crisis of authority within the GDR, which could then be exploited by internal dissenters'. The build-up of long-term political, social and economic structural problems in the GDR (see pages 117–23) combined with the weakening of the government's authority when support from the USSR was withdrawn. This allowed dissent to be increasingly openly voiced. The summer of 1989 saw mass demonstrations and the growth of opposition movements, which further challenged the authority and legitimacy of the East German government.

Events in the summer of 1989 outside the GDR
Growing migration from the GDR

Changes taking place in Hungary encouraged dissent within the GDR and also led to the return of mass emigration from the GDR. Hungary had been introducing reforms in the late 1980s and by 1989 was allowing multi-party elections. This was a serious concern to the GDR government as Hungary was a popular holiday destination for many East Germans, and ideas about reform might influence their own citizens. They also feared that the nationalism which inspired much of the Hungarian reform movement might encourage demands from GDR opposition movements for the reuniting of Germany.

On 2 May 1989, the reforming Hungarian government opened its border with Austria, an event which James McAdams calls 'the beginning of the end of the GDR'. By the summer, more than 30,000 East Germans used the newly opened Hungarian border to cross from the GDR into the FRG via Hungary and Austria. This emigration intensified in the autumn, with East Germans inundating West German embassies in Prague and Warsaw; the numbers leaving the GDR reached over 100,000. Under West German law, they could claim FRG passports once in Austria. Many of these were exactly the sort of people that the GDR could ill afford to lose. At this stage, the majority were young, male, single workers with jobs in industry and transport, although a significant number had qualifications in medicine and teaching. This was in contrast to those who tended to remain and protest inside the GDR. Those who stayed were predominantly students and those with parents working for the SED, government officials and managers in industry. Such people were less inclined to leave the GDR since many of them had the prospect of fulfilling careers. They were generally more dissatisfied with restrictions on daily life and travel.

The treatment that East Germans who had decided to leave via Hungary received once in the FRG encouraged even more to emigrate. They were enthusiastically welcomed into West German resettlement camps and given offers of employment and housing. The situation worsened for the East German government when, on 11 September, the Hungarian government announced it would now legally allow any East Germans to cross its border into neutral Austria (before this date East Germans could have been arrested, although none had been); this was a severe blow to Honecker from a supposed Warsaw Pact ally. On 3 October, in an attempt to stem the rapidly rising tide of emigration, the GDR closed its border with Czechoslovakia. It also made it more difficult for East Germans to cross the border into Poland. But by this stage thousands of refugees had already left the GDR and were camping in the grounds of the West German embassies in Prague and Warsaw. Honecker allowed them exit visas and provided sealed trains to transport them from Poland and Czechoslovakia through the GDR to the FRG. The image of a nation imprisoning its own population was then further reinforced by the scenes at Dresden train station when thousands

Key question
How did reforms in Hungary affect the GDR?

Reforming Hungarian government opened its border with Austria: 2 May 1989

Key date

more unsuccessfully attempted to board the trains. Pictures filled the screens of Western news programmes, and of course reached viewers in the GDR.

Developments on the international scene

Key question
How did events on the international scene influence developments in the GDR?

At the same time as domestic events were starting to prove a serious challenge to the GDR's leadership, there were also significant developments in the international scene that further increased the GDR government's vulnerability. In the summer of 1989, the USA appeared to be reassessing its policy towards Europe. When US President Bush visited the FRG for the 40th anniversary of NATO he stated that the USA sought '**self-determination** for all of Germany and all of Eastern Europe … the world has waited long enough'. At the same time, the USSR was suggesting further arms reductions, including the withdrawal of 500 short-range nuclear weapons from the GDR. Gorbachev was also greeted enthusiastically during a visit to the FRG in June 1989. During the visit, Kohl stated that his aim was for the eventual reuniting of Germany, even if was not going to happen during his own lifetime.

Key term

Self-determination
The right of nations to govern themselves, free from control by another power.

The growth of opposition in the GDR
Gorbachev's example in the USSR

Key question
Why did opposition grow in the summer of 1989?

The policies being followed by Gorbachev inside the USSR were in direct contrast to those of the East German government. Honecker was intent on maintaining hard-line socialist control and had tightened repression and censorship during 1988 and 1989 (see page 122). In contrast, the USSR had begun to ease press censorship and introduce radical economic reforms. The example set by Gorbachev undermined Honecker's hard-line stance and encouraged challenges to it.

Local election results

Key date

Opposition groups in the GDR monitored local election results: 7 May 1989

The public protests began on 7 May 1989 when opposition groups in the GDR monitored local election results. They condemned what they saw as the government's deliberate exaggeration of the results to make it appear that the SED-dominated National Front had won 99 per cent of the vote. These results were widely seen as fraudulent and the demonstrations that followed in East Berlin led to the arrest of over 100 protestors.

Reactions to Tiananmen Square

In June 1989, many inside East Germany were angered by the GDR government's attitude to the protests for democratic reforms in China. The GDR government congratulated the Chinese communist government's tough treatment of protestors in Tiananmen Square, Beijing. Television sets around the world showed shocking pictures of tanks being used against the unarmed demonstrators. Between 200 and 2000 Chinese demonstrators were killed. The GDR government's decision to applaud the Chinese government's tough response may have been intended by the East German authorities to serve as a grave warning to those in the GDR on the possible repercussions if they themselves demonstrated. However, the effect of the implied threat was to intensify resentment within the GDR itself.

New groups and the growth of protest

- During the summer of 1989 opposition groups became more vocal in the GDR. Their new confidence was undoubtedly encouraged by to the political developments in the USSR and other Eastern bloc states, such as Solidarity's success in Poland in August 1989. In the GDR, opposition groups began demonstrating on issues such as human rights, free elections, freedom of the press and assembly, and freedom to travel. Dissent increasingly moved out into the open, no longer contained within the tolerated church discussion framework. New political groups were formed, openly committed to working for political change.
- In July, the East German Social Democratic Party was formed (renamed SPD from January 1990).
- In August a group called 'Democratic Reawakening' was formed, which was to become a political party in late October.
- Democracy Now was set up in August 1989, mainly made up of intellectuals.
- The group that emerged as the most influential was New Forum, which sought to create a broad-based appeal. New Forum deliberately aimed to challenge the ruling SED.

It is easy to assume that the opposition groups were calling for the end to the separate existence of the GDR. This is far from the case. New Forum's manifesto was focused on securing greater freedom within the GDR itself rather than on encouraging emigration to the FRG. Its aim was a reformed GDR. And even as the challenges to the East German government grew, some opposition groups' leaders were already concerned about the possible effects if Germany were reunified. The leader of Democracy Now, Konrad Weiss, expressed grave concerns that the GDR would end up as a 'state' which would simply be annexed to an enlarged FRG.

Increasing internal dissent in the GDR

During the summer Honecker himself was largely off stage, owing to a gallbladder operation (he was later diagnosed with cancer). But by the autumn of 1989 the East German government was faced with two forms of damaging popular protest: those who emigrated were clearly voting against the regime with their feet, while those who remained to protest inside the GDR became increasingly bold. Over the autumn both these forms of protest grew. From the very outset, the internal protest groups advocated non-violent means to achieve their aims. Consequently, this period from mid-1989 onwards is often referred to as Germany's 'peaceful revolution'. Both the opposition groups and the authorities declined to use force.

Round Table
A group set up in
December 1989
with members from
both the East
German
Volkskammer and
opposition groups
to discuss
government
policies.

However, in spite of the numbers involved, the strength of opposition at this stage was limited by the difficulties it faced. Although the various groups shared some common principles and values, it was very hard for them to liaise with each other and campaign in a united and concerted way because of continued *Stasi* surveillance. Nevertheless, some of these organisations were later to play an important role in the setting up of the **Round Table** which was to participate in the first free East German elections in March 1990.

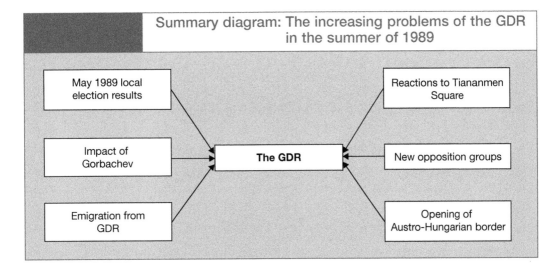

Summary diagram: The increasing problems of the GDR in the summer of 1989

2 | The Events Leading to the Opening of the Berlin Wall

The position of the East German government weakened during October and November 1989 as challenges from below were finally met by a collapse of authority from above. Events inside the GDR and circumstances outside combined to compromise the government's strength and its authority. As in the 1950s, the mass emigration seriously weakened the legitimacy of the East German government as well as damaging the practical day-to-day functioning of the state. These were the very same factors, 30 years previously, that had faced the GDR before the building of the Berlin Wall. However, the fundamental difference in 1989 was the absence of any support from the USSR.

Gorbachev visited
East Berlin for the
GDR's 40th
anniversary
celebrations:
6 October 1989

Gorbachev's visit to East Berlin

On 6 October the Soviet leader Gorbachev was in East Berlin for the 40th anniversary celebrations of the founding of the GDR. A few days earlier the Soviet Foreign Minister had warned Eastern European governments that if they refused to follow the USSR's lead in adopting extensive reforms there would undoubtedly be a mass exodus from Eastern Europe. The 40th celebrations took place against a backdrop of domestic demonstrations with up to 1000 arrests in East Berlin, with the public chanting 'Gorby help us'. Simultaneously, Gorbachev was urging Honecker to implement reforms similar to those undertaken by many other Eastern European governments, and warning of the dangers of acting too late. He also made it clear that the USSR was unwilling to intervene directly on the East German government's behalf. Gorbachev was also not prepared to devote resources to sustaining the GDR since this would be a major handicap to his own Soviet reform programme. Crawshaw has suggested that the GDR's 40th anniversary was 'intended to be a glorious set of celebrations, and was instead … a funeral wake'.

Honecker's response to the growing demonstrations and mass emigration

Gorbachev's explicit refusal to give any direct support to Honecker gave added impetus to those demonstrating. The protestors in the GDR were demanding change on many similar issues to those which were being fought for, and won, in other Eastern European states. However, the vital difference for East German protestors was Honecker's intransigence. He was adamant that the East German government would maintain socialist rule and he was therefore unwilling to implement any reforms. The critical dilemma for East German leaders was how could they ever explain or justify the existence of 'another Germany' if both Germanys were based on the same political and economic principles. Honecker returned to the political scene in late September after his operation; in many ways his return made matters much worse for the SED. He blamed the FRG for the GDR's problems and on 2 October he ordered the official SED newspaper *Neues Deutschland* to publish a statement denouncing those emigrating from the GDR as 'counter-revolutionaries'.

Honecker's own intransigence at this point was a significant link in the chain of events leading to the downfall of the very regime he was so determined to preserve. Historian James McAdams notes that the speed of East Germany's collapse might possibly have been slower if the SED Politburo members who finally removed Honecker in October 1989 had acted two months earlier. The government which replaced Honecker's in the second part of October offered travel concessions and showed a greater readiness to consider the political reforms that the protestors were demanding. But, by then, it was not enough. Gorbachev's remark that 'Life punishes those who come too late' proved to be only too accurate.

Demonstrations at the St Nikolai Church, Leipzig

In the late 1980s reform groups had started to emerge based around the churches in Leipzig, especially the St Nikolai Church. Here peace prayers had been held every Monday evening since the early 1980s. From the spring of 1989, the church services had often been followed by a small public rally. But the political changes in other Eastern bloc states, and the growing numbers

Key question
Why were the Leipzig demonstrations significant?

emigrating from the GDR, increased the frequency and size of these popular demonstrations. The weekly gatherings significantly increased in size during the autumn of 1989. On the last Monday in September thousands filled the streets to parade peacefully and sing protest songs.

Leipzig demonstration 9 October 1989

By Monday 9 October there were over 70,000 demonstrators. The government had prepared additional armed forces, and special *Stasi* units were put on alert. Many East Germans were convinced that, since Honecker lacked support from the USSR, he would not risk using force. Nevertheless, the lack of any intervention by the authorities was a welcome relief and came as a surprise to many. The only response by the East German government on 9 October was to block West German radio signals and to refuse Westerners entry into East Berlin. Soviet forces stationed in the GDR remained firmly inside their barracks. Apparently, Honecker himself and his secret police chief had advocated repression, and a 'China solution' (see page 129) was debated in East German government circles. Honecker had even arranged for extra doctors and blood supplies to be sent to Leipzig. Severe violence and bloodshed were avoided by only a narrow margin. In the event, Honecker refrained from using force. His decision seems to have been prompted by a combination of fear of triggering a civil war and fear that the GDR's security forces could not be relied on if ordered to move against the peaceful demonstration.

The lack of intervention by the East German army, police force or *Stasi* gave future demonstrators even more courage and determination. Historian Mike Dennis observes '9 October was a decisive turning point as it exposed the political bankruptcy of the SED hardliners'. Demonstrations spread to other parts of the GDR, notably Dresden and Berlin. At this stage the popular protests were advocating change and reform within the GDR and not the reunification of Germany. There was frequent chanting of '*Wir sind das Volk*' ('We are the people') and '*Wir bleiben hier*' ('We are staying here'). The demands were largely concerned with issues such as freedom of the press, assembly, travel, an end to the *Stasi*, free elections and action on environmental issues. Church leaders strongly urged protestors to remain non-violent.

Honecker's resignation

The demonstrations, emigration and Honecker's refusal to reform did, however, give SED leaders the impetus to replace him. Honecker could not call on Soviet support. Gorbachev firmly stated that this was entirely an internal matter for the GDR's own government to resolve, and he continued to maintain the policy of Soviet non-intervention in the internal affairs of Eastern bloc states. On 17 October the East German Politburo asked for Honecker to be removed and to be replaced by Egon Krenz, another member of the Politburo. The following day, Honecker, realising the inevitable, requested that he be allowed to step down

Key question
Why did Honecker resign?

Key date
Honecker resigned and was replaced by Krenz as General Secretary of the SED: 18 October 1989

on health grounds. Krenz duly replaced him as General Secretary of the SED.

Krenz's attempts at reform

Krenz was by no means fully supported by all of the Politburo. It was clear that under his leadership, the East German government would attempt to preserve the SED's dominant role, in spite of the continuing demonstrations which explicitly included demands for free elections. On 24 October Krenz offered free travel, believing naïvely that this would be sufficient to appease the protestors. Krenz also agreed to meet church leaders and representatives from New Forum. Simultaneously, a propaganda campaign was launched. *Neues Deutschland* ran articles on social issues in the FRG, such as homelessness and the cheating of recent GDR emigrants. A week later, in another attempt to quell the rising tide of demonstrations, Krenz tried a political reshuffle. He removed other key figures associated with the Honecker regime: Mielke (head of the *Stasi*), Hager (Mayor of Leipzig) and Honecker's wife, Margot (Minister for Education). They were replaced with new and younger faces.

Krenz's reforms, however, had the opposite effect to the one he had anticipated. Concessions only increased the opposition's

Key question
Why did Krenz's reforms fail?

Demonstrations on Alexanderplatz in East Berlin, 4 November 1989. This was the largest demonstration in the GDR and was broadcast live on GDR television.

Key date

Monday demonstrators in Leipzig chanted 'Germany – One Fatherland': 6 November 1989

appetite for more. On 4 November the largest demonstration in German history took place in East Berlin, with over a million people attending. On 6 November half a million demonstrators marched in Leipzig. They demanded new travel laws and an end to the SED's monopoly on power, but, significantly chants were also heard for 'Germany – One Fatherland'. As it transpired, early November demonstrations were to be the last which primarily demanded reform within the GDR rather than reunification with the FRG. In response to the growth in public demonstrations and also pressure from the Czech government, which was worried about destabilisation on its border with the GDR, Krenz made further concessions. On 6 November he promised all East Germans passports and the freedom to travel for up to 30 days a year. On 9 November an SED working party recommended that any GDR citizen with a passport or visa could emigrate or visit the West. It was planned to announce this on the following day, 10 November. However, a simple misunderstanding led to the most dramatic and, arguably, the single most symbolic event in the process of the reuniting of the two Germanys happening on 9 November 1989, 24 hours earlier than was intended.

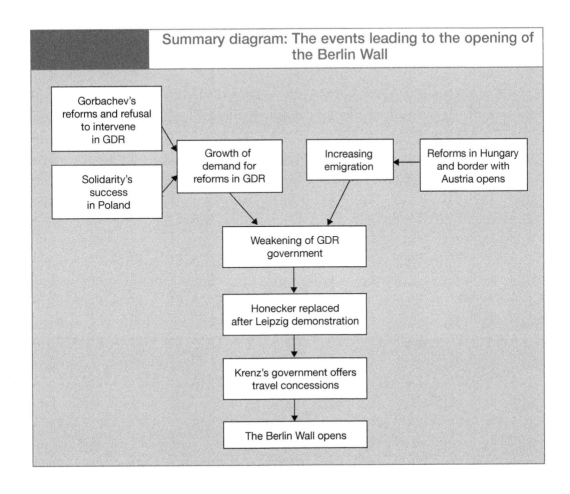

Summary diagram: The events leading to the opening of the Berlin Wall

3 | November 1989: The Opening of the Berlin Wall and its Immediate Impact

Key question
What was the immediate response to the opening of the Berlin Wall?

Even in the early autumn of 1989 the idea of West Germans and East Germans standing and celebrating with each other on the top of the Berlin Wall would have been unthinkable. Yet to the amazement of many, and to the alarm of some world leaders, this is exactly what was witnessed in person and on television screens across the world on the night of 9 November 1989. This began a rapid chain of events which led, in less than a year, to the formal reuniting of Germany in October 1990 and the USSR's acceptance of reunited Germany as a member of an enlarged NATO. Within less than two years the wall was almost entirely dismantled and today only a few parts of the wall and sections of the 'inner-German border' remain standing. They serve as memorials and historical monuments to a divided nation which had epitomised the Cold War, by existing either side of a heavily fortified 'iron curtain' for nearly half a century.

The opening of the Berlin Wall

On 9 November unrestricted travel from the GDR to the FRG was announced and parts of the Berlin Wall were opened. The GDR Politburo, led by Krenz, had decided to allow travel directly between East and West Germany at a number of crossing points, including Berlin. They felt that by liberalising the travel laws they would keep GDR citizens at home; the would-be emigrants would cross the newly opened border, take one look at the West, and then simply return home. It was originally intended that the opening would be delayed until the next day to give sufficient time to instruct the East German border guards. The SED leader for East Berlin, Günther Schabowski, was to make the announcement. However, he had not been properly prepared and

Key date
Unrestricted travel from the GDR to the FRG announced and parts of the Berlin Wall opened: 9 November 1989

Opening of the wall, November 1989. East German border guards dwarfed by a crowd waiting to cross into West Berlin.

at a press conference that same evening he read out a note given to him and assumed that the opening of crossing points was for the very same day rather than the following day. With some hesitation, he responded to a question about the timing of the opening of the Berlin Wall by answering that it would take immediate effect.

To the astonishment of both East and West Germans, the evening's main item on the 8 p.m. news on West German television was 'the GDR opens its borders'. Within the next few hours thousands of East Berliners flooded the checkpoints demanding entry into West Berlin. The border guards, who had received no formal instructions, were completely unable to hold back the vast crowds and opened the checkpoints to let people through. By midnight, the GDR police announced that all border crossing points between East and West Berlin had been opened.

The initial euphoria in both Germanys

Key question
How did Germans on both sides react initially to the opening of the Berlin Wall?

Ecstatic East and West Berliners met in celebration. The day of this historic event – 9 November – was later suggested as a date for a new national holiday, German Unity Day. However, 3 October was chosen instead, largely because 9 November, by a twist of historical coincidence, was also the date of the proclamation of the Weimar Republic in 1918, Hitler's Munich Beer Hall *Putsch* in 1923 and *Kristallnacht* in 1938. Since then, inside Germany, 9 November has been termed 'day of fate' and judged unsuitable for a German national celebration.

Germans from both sides climbed up and danced on the wall. Some amazed East Berliners crossed in their pyjamas, and formerly unapproachable East German border guards were kissed by East Germans as they crossed the border, while some border troops were seen with flowers protruding from their rifle barrels. The first weekend that GDR citizens could freely enter West Berlin they were greeted with free gifts such as beer, tickets to football matches and access to public transport. West Berliners gave out chocolate, champagne and fresh fruit (bananas and grapes had rarely been seen, let alone eaten, in East Germany.) East Germans also received DM100 as 'welcome money', which, although important as a gesture, could actually purchase relatively little, just a few basic meals and drinks. This was not mass emigration. Most who crossed the border to celebrate the new freedom to travel simply returned back home to the GDR at this point. But it prompted a large number to start making plans or give serious thought to moving west over the following few months. This would severely strain the GDR's already fragile economy and place heavy burdens on the FRG's welfare system and taxation levels.

In effect, the opening of the wall meant that there was now no turning back for the GDR government. It could not reverse the concessions it had made, even if socialist power lingered on. But at this stage, the wall was being opened, not dismantled. The reunification of Germany was not yet a foregone conclusion. It seemed that some of the SED regime thought that the opening of the wall would calm the domestic situation inside the GDR. German nationalism, however, had by now become a distinct feature of the popular mood, and there were increased calls for reunification. The lure of Western prosperity was also strong. Anthony Glees remarks that the demonstrators were now motivated by 'the wish for Western liberty and the *Deutschmark*'. The future course of events now largely depended on the responses from the FRG and its Chancellor, Helmut Kohl, and from the four Allied powers of the Second World War coalition.

The East German leadership's attempts at reform

By the end of 1989, the East German government had undergone a revolution: first, with the overthrow of Honecker and then with the surrender of the SED's monopoly of power. The process of revolutionary change had been accomplished mainly by the behaviour of SED members in the *Volkskammer* themselves and by the actions of the rank-and-file membership of the SED party in the GDR at large. The old leadership was deprived of office and even of parliamentary seats. In December the *Volkskammer* actually voted to end the constitutional position which had given the SED political dominance. Throughout the GDR many SED Party officials were removed. Censorship was lifted at the end of November, and the old establishment's authority was further weakened. The SED reorganised and renamed itself the SED-PDS: Socialist Unity Party of Germany and Party of Democratic Socialism. It soon became known as the PDS.

Krenz was too closely associated with the previous regime to survive. Protestors demonstrated against him on the streets, and he resigned after only 44 days in office. The power structures changed rapidly within the GDR. The SED-dominated Politburo and the Central Committee were abolished and power passed to the Council of Ministers. Hans Modrow, one of the SED's regional party chiefs, became Prime Minister. Modrow was known to be a reformer. Indeed, it seems Gorbachev would have preferred him to have been appointed earlier, instead of Krenz. The new government announced free elections, a state based on the rule of law and economic reforms.

Thus, in only a few months at the end of 1989 a peaceful revolution had occurred in the GDR. Remarkably, it had been achieved without central direction or a charismatic leading figure. It had been driven by the people of the GDR by sheer weight of numbers, not by violent disruption. It had swept away the controls which had existed ever since the GDR had come into being. In the early months of 1990 plans for reform were agreed by the Round Table and government ministers. It was clear that the old authoritarian structure of the GDR had been transformed. By early February, eight former opposition members were now part of the government.

However, these reforms proved insufficient to preserve the GDR's independent existence. The explanation for this lies in the continuing tide of emigration. Estimates put this as high as

Key question
What attempts at reform were made in the GDR?

Key date

Constitutional change in GDR ended supreme role of the SED: 1 December 1989

75,000 in January 1990 alone. Such large numbers were putting the East German economy under unsustainable strain. The emigrants were those groups – young workers – that the state could least afford to lose. East Germans would increasingly turn up for school, to work or for an appointment, to find that individuals had simply left. The flight of its people contributed to the GDR's economic slump, which in turn weakened the GDR politically. The mass emigration fatally compromised the legitimacy of the GDR as a state. It also influenced government policy in the FRG, which became increasingly anxious to stem the tide of migration which was threatening its own economy.

Reactions in the FRG to the opening of the wall

Key question
What problems did emigration from the GDR cause the FRG in the period 1989–90?

In November, Kohl, the West German Chancellor, stated that it was in the East Germans' best interests to stay inside the GDR. He promised assistance on condition that the SED gave up total control. It is clear that Kohl was treading very carefully at this point. With two million East Germans flooding into the FRG, he was concerned to safeguard the interests of the FRG and its electorate. The influx of easterners into the FRG placed an immense strain on housing, welfare provision and employment in the FRG. Other influential figures in the FRG favoured reform and modernisation within the GDR in order to reduce emigration:

- The SPD Mayor of West Berlin, Walter Momper, supported Kohl's policy of assistance to the GDR.
- The former West German SPD Chancellor, Helmut Schmidt, promoted the idea of a special tax to support modernisation of the GDR. In many ways this can be seen as a logical extension of the policy of *Ostpolitik*.
- Wolfgang Vogel of the West German SPD urged East Germans to remain inside the GDR and work towards reform.

Kohl's Ten-Point Plan for Germany

Key question
What was the significance of Kohl's Ten-Point Plan?

Key date
Kohl announced his 'Ten-Point Plan': 28 November 1989

At this point Kohl's own intervention was significant. On 28 November, acting entirely on his own initiative, without any consultation with the Western Allies, or from his FDP coalition partners, Kohl announced his Ten-Point Plan which included proposals for economic aid to the GDR and practical improvements such as more efficient postal services. But it also dropped a bombshell. It contained proposals for the reuniting of Germany by a confederation of the GDR and the FRG. The plan also included proposals for creating the conditions that were necessary before the new federation could be formed. It demanded an end to the SED's monopoly on power, free elections, the dismantling of the GDR's socialist economy and its replacement with a market economy. But this was not to be a hurried affair. According to the German historian Gerhard Wettig, Kohl still believed, at this stage, that reunification would take four to five years to complete. In spite of its long-term

---

Profile: Helmut Kohl 1930–

1930	– Born in Ludwigshafen am Rhein
1945	– Conscripted in the very final weeks of the Second World War but was not involved in any actual fighting
1946	– Joined the CDU
1982–90	– CDU Chancellor of the FRG
1990–8	– CDU Chancellor of a newly reunited Germany

Kohl's leadership of the FRG from 1982 to 1990, and then of a reunited Germany from 1990 to 1998, made him the longest serving German Chancellor since Bismarck. His period of office saw the continuation of *Ostpolitik* and the state visit of Honecker, the first of a GDR leader to the FRG, in 1987. By the late 1980s, support for Kohl was falling, but the sudden events of 1989–90 changed his political fortunes. His handling of the immediate period following the opening of the Berlin Wall in November 1989 was arguably the culmination of *Ostpolitik* and led to his being regarded by many as the 'unification Chancellor'. He was, however, subject to intense criticism after his retirement from politics when it emerged that under his leadership the CDU had received illegal funding. In addition, there was controversy surrounding his refusal to have the contents of his *Stasi* file revealed.

---

nature and the lack of a precise timetable, Kohl's plan electrified the reunification debate both in Germany and internationally. Lothar Kettenacker observes 'the international community could not ignore the crucial issue which hitherto had only been a battle cry in the streets of Europe'.

Mixed reactions to Kohl's plan

At this stage, such a proposal was far too sudden for the USSR which was concerned by the possibility of a reunited Germany's membership of NATO. Margaret Thatcher, the British Prime Minister, was also anxious and alarmed at the thought of an enlarged Germany, and some British tabloid newspapers fuelled fears of a resurgent, all-too powerful Germany, while the French press talked of a fourth *Reich*. Jacques Delors, President of the European Commission, suggested that the GDR should become a member of the European Union as a second German state. In the GDR, Modrow as Prime Minister was advocating a 'third way' involving the preservation of the GDR a separate state. However, US President Bush, in an interview with the *New York Times*, stated that he would welcome a unified Germany.

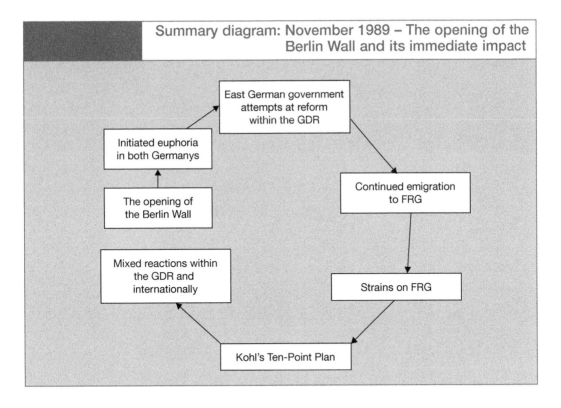

Summary diagram: November 1989 – The opening of the Berlin Wall and its immediate impact

4 | The Disintegration of the GDR

The failure of attempts to preserve the East German regime

Key question
Why did reform in the GDR fail to stop the flood of emigration?

The reforms offered by the East German government were having little effect on the situation. In December, demonstrations called for a 'united Fatherland'. The chants had shifted from '*Wir sind das Volk*' ('We are the people') to '*Wir sind ein Volk*' ('We are one people'). Despite the opening of the Berlin Wall and freedom to travel, many GDR citizens continued to leave the GDR for the West. The East German crisis had two key aspects:

- The attractions of Western consumer society were fuelled by the experience of East Germans visiting West Berlin.
- Opposition was strengthened by a significant number of 'new' protestors who now felt confident to join the demonstrations. Opposition to the government of the GDR brought with it much less risk to personal safety than they had feared before November 1989 and before the opening of the Berlin Wall.

From December onwards the demonstrations were increasingly supportive of German reunification and were rapidly shifting away from a 'third way' solution. On 22 December 1989, Berlin's symbolic Brandenburg Gate was opened, and on a hugely emotional Christmas Day in 1989, the American conductor Leonard Bernstein led an orchestra in a performance of Beethoven's ninth symphony with its Ode to Joy finale changed to Ode to Freedom. The chorus was made up from singers from

New Year's Eve 1989 at the Brandenburg Gate in central Berlin. The banner reads 'Germany one Fatherland'.

Germany, the USA, France, the UK and the USSR. The public mood was such that, by the spring of 1990, it was becoming obvious that an independent and democratic GDR was increasingly unlikely to survive.

The impact of lessening control

As controls on information weakened, revelations within the GDR added to its growing problems. This was especially apparent with the increasing awareness of economic problems in the GDR, environmental concerns, and the extent and activities of the *Stasi*.

Key question
Why did the GDR government continue to lose support?

On 15 January 1990 a protest took place at the *Stasi* headquarters in East Berlin. Members of the *Stasi* had frantically been trying to destroy as much paperwork as possible. The demonstrators were demanding that the files should be kept for use later as evidence to prosecute *Stasi* employees. The storming of the building included the smashing of furniture and windows, and the tearing down of portraits of Honecker.

Files retrieved later showed that prominent figures in the SPD, Democratic Reawakening and the church had been collaborating as IMs with the *Stasi*. The records show that there had been a deliberate policy of planting *Stasi* officers inside the reform groups with the aim of trying to curtail the various groups' activities and to gather key information. The extent of *Stasi* operations within the opposition groups has also led to theories that the *Stasi* were deliberately encouraging dissent to topple Honecker, perhaps even with support from Gorbachev, in order to preserve the GDR. But this speculation is dismissed by historian Mary Fulbrook as being 'a little far-fetched'.

Key question
What were the main issues for the first free election in the GDR?

Key date

Free elections to the GDR parliament held: 18 March 1990

The first free elections in the GDR, March 1990

Following the change in the constitution of the GDR that diminished the role of the SED, free elections were initially scheduled for May 1990. The timing of the elections, however, was brought forward to March in view of the growing domestic crisis. The economic problems became more pronounced with the increasing emigration, strikes and the emergence of a black economy. The election campaign was dominated by debate over the various policies put forward by political parties regarding the future of the GDR. By early 1990, Modrow, the Round Table and most other GDR groups had come to accept German reunification, as had the West German SPD. By March, Gorbachev had publicly accepted the principle of the unification of Germany, although the question of its NATO membership remained uncertain. The main differences between the political parties rested on the speed with which unification was to be accomplished and the extent to which existing elements of the GDR socialist system would be preserved.

For the vast majority of GDR citizens, the March 1990 elections were the first free elections for nearly 60 years, although any fascist or militarist groups were banned from standing. Table 5.1 summarises the main programme of the various groups campaigning in the elections and the number of seats they gained.

The euphoria that accompanied the election was evident in the huge crowds flocking to see and hear the West German politicians

East Germans demonstrating in March 1990. The banner reads 'If the *Deutschmark* comes, we stay here – otherwise we go to it'.

Table 5.1: The March 1990 GDR election

Political party/group	Policy	Number of seats gained
PDS (the renamed SED)	Wanted to keep socialism and much of the existing economic organisation of the GDR, but accepted the principle of the eventual linking of the two Germanys.	66
The Alliance for Germany, dominated by the CDU	Favoured the fastest route towards complete reunification. This would absorb the East German *Länder* into the existing FRG and mean the rapid adoption of a market economy.	192
SPD	Wanted reunification but at a slower pace by creating a new constitution for a newly reunited Germany, which in effect, would be more of a joint merger of the GDR and the FRG.	87

who campaigned in support of their East German political allies. Kohl himself campaigned energetically and was received enthusiastically in the GDR. In Leipzig, he addressed a crowd of a million people. The election result was a clear and decisive vote for the CDU's policy of swift change and the rapid introduction into the GDR of the West German *Deutschmark*, which was associated with economic stability and prosperity. The Alliance gained 48 per cent of the vote. Konrad Jarausch attributes much of this to Kohl, whose 'vague promises created a blinding national euphoria, and the fearful masses embraced hope'. Faced by the deepening economic crisis in the GDR, voters were attracted by the strength of the *Deutschmark* and the notion of becoming *Ein Volk* ('one people') again. The proposals for more gradual reform of the GDR itself went largely unheard in the climate of enthusiasm and optimism generated by Kohl and the 'Alliance for Germany'.

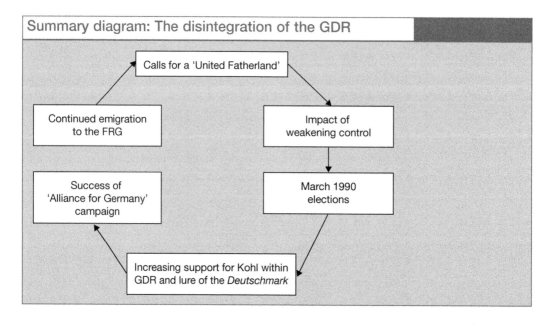

Summary diagram: The disintegration of the GDR

5 | The Process of Reuniting the GDR and the FRG

Economic unity

Key question
What impact did economic unity have on the GDR's economy?

Key date
Currency union between the FRG and the GDR: 1 July 1990

The first stage of reunification was economic union. This was needed urgently in the context of the spiralling economic difficulties within the GDR. In May 1990, Kohl signed an economic and social union treaty with the GDR. Further, in spite of the West German *Bundesbank*'s reservations, he implemented a one-to-one currency conversion between East German and West German marks, which included salaries, wages and pensions. Kohl's policy was based on his perception that a new currency and the introduction of market forces in the FRG in 1948–51 had led to the economic recovery and the economic boom of the 1950s and 1960s. This currency union between the FRG and the GDR took place on 1 July. However, it resulted in the GDR's economy quickly collapsing and left many East German citizens financially worse off. Demand for East German goods fell sharply as economic union made Western consumer goods readily available and removed the subsidies which had allowed East German goods to be sold cheaply in both East and West.

By mid-summer, 20 per cent of the GDR's workforce was either unemployed or reduced to part-time employment. Strikes and demonstrations were becoming more frequent and the complete bankruptcy of the GDR was only staved off by huge financial subsidies from Bonn. With its outdated machinery and over-high staffing levels, industry and agriculture in the GDR were simply uncompetitive. East German farmers were particularly hard hit. Their subsidies had gone and they faced stiff economic competition from the FRG and the EEC. Over 250,000 farmers demonstrated in August and constructed street blockades. The effect of economic union was to convince many in both East and West Germany that only speedy and full unification could deal with the rapidly deteriorating economic position.

Discussions with the Allied powers

Key term
Two plus Four
The two Germanys and the four powers from the Second World War.

Discussions and agreements made between the GDR and FRG alone could not lead to reunification. This could only occur with the support and agreement from the four Second World War Allied powers. Full negotiations needed to take place between the West German government and the USSR, the USA, France and the UK. '**Two plus Four**' negotiations took place from May to September 1990. Much of the discussion centred on what relationship a newly united Germany would have with NATO. The key players in the decision-making were the USA and the USSR, and one important factor in the outcome was the relationship Kohl developed with the two superpowers.

The FRG's relations with the USA

Kohl had previously developed closer West German relations with the USA. In 1985, Kohl and US President Reagan used the 40th anniversary of the end of the Second World War in Europe as an opportunity to display German–American co-operation and reconciliation. As part of a visit to West Germany, Reagan visited the former Nazi concentration camp at Bergen-Belsen and also a German military cemetery at Bitburg. The latter unfortunately caused Kohl a great deal of political embarrassment as the cemetery marks the site where up to 50 Nazi SS officers were buried. As part of a commitment to German–American relations, Reagan also visited West Berlin in 1987 and made a famous speech at the site of the Brandenburg Gate with the now famous line: 'Mr Gorbachev tear down this wall!' The US President in 1990, George Bush, was fully behind reunification. British and French opposition was soon reduced by Kohl's commitment to a policy of a reunited Germany's membership both of NATO and the EEC.

Negotiations with the USSR

The harder task was to secure the consent of the USSR. Ever since the end of the Second World War, Soviet foreign policy had been concerned to preserve a buffer between the West and its own borders, in the form of either a satellite state or a neutral state. Only in the climate of the reduction in Cold War tensions was it possible for the Soviet leader even to contemplate this extension of NATO power and influence with the prospect of the presence of NATO troops in the former GDR. On 16 July 1990, a historic meeting between Kohl and Gorbachev resolved the remaining issues. Gorbachev agreed to Kohl's plan for full reunification and to a reunited Germany's membership of NATO. On the key issue of troop deployment it was agreed that no foreign forces would be placed in the territory of the former GDR and Kohl agreed to fund the withdrawal of Soviet troops from the GDR. Kohl also promised to pay the USSR DM12 billion for housing and other resettlement work in the USSR on behalf of the returning Soviet soldiers. (Interestingly, some Soviet soldiers wrote personal letters to Kohl asking him to delay their deployment back to the USSR.) Their withdrawal was to be completed by 1994. The dire state of the USSR's own economy and the financial strength of the FRG were significant factors in reducing Soviet opposition to the issue of a reunited Germany's membership of NATO.

The Unification Treaty

The Unification Treaty was signed by the GDR and FRG on 31 August 1990. It was agreed that on reunification on 3 October, the re-established pre-war *Länder* of the GDR would become *Länder* of the FRG. The final Two-plus-Four Treaty was signed on 12 September in Moscow. The four wartime Allies officially gave up all formal rights they held in the two Germanys and the city of Berlin. The newly reunited Germany agreed to the size of its combined armed forces being no more than 370,000 and in particular agreed that the Nuclear Non-Proliferation Treaty would be honoured. The treaty also laid down that no foreign forces or nuclear weapons would be placed in the former GDR territory.

Key question
What issues were at stake in the negotiations between Kohl and Gorbachev?

Key dates
USSR agreed to a reunited Germany being part of NATO: 16 July 1990

Final Two-plus-Four Treaty signed in Moscow: September 1990

Key question
What were the main aspects of the Unification Treaty?

Kohl also had to settle some other long-standing issues with the former wartime Allies. Any German territorial claims to the east of the Oder–Neisse line (part of Poland since 1945) were ended and a separate treaty was signed with Poland in November. Later, in 1993, in an agreement with the Czech Republic, Kohl renounced any German territorial claims to the pre-1945 Sudetenland.

Unification

Key dates

GDR was abolished and its territory was formally reunited with the FRG: 3 October 1990

The first post-war all-German election returned Kohl as Chancellor: December 1990

The final dismantling of the Berlin Wall: November 1991

The GDR was abolished on 3 October 1990 and its territory was formally reunited with the FRG. The official speeches at the Brandenburg Gate were noticeably much more solemn in tone than they had been at the opening of the very same site only 10 months before. The reformed GDR had lasted less than a year before its territory became new *Länder* of an enlarged FRG. Konrad Jarausch and Volker Gransow describe this as a process by which 'the GDR simply dissolved itself, and its component states joined the FRG'. Since unification 3 October has been an official German national holiday called the 'Day of German Unity'. Over the next few weeks parts of the Berlin Wall were increasingly broken up by ordinary people wielding hammers and chisels. The wall was later knocked down using industrial equipment, although it took until late 1991 for the final dismantling to be completed. The dismantling process was symbolic of a new German unity. It involved the co-operation of the former East German army with British and former West German soldiers.

The first all-German election, December 1990

In December 1990 the first post-war all-German election returned Kohl as Chancellor with a landslide victory. Forty-four per cent of the vote went to the CDU/CSU, 34 per cent to the SPD, 11 per cent to the FDP, and a mere two per cent to the PDS (the former SED). Kohl's CDU, in coalition with the FDP, controlled 398 of the 662 seats in the new *Bundestag*. The size of the CDU/CSU vote can be seen as the German public's endorsement of Kohl's unification policy. He formed his fourth cabinet with promises of 'blooming landscapes' and 'economic wonders'. These were soon seen to have been hugely optimistic or, as some might argue, purposefully misleading.

Key question
Why did problems emerge so soon after the reuniting of Germany?

Early signs of disillusionment

The sheer speed of these changes, and the process by which the GDR basically became the new *Länder* of the FRG, surprised and shocked many both inside Germany and further afield. The new united Germany faced fresh internal challenges. The initial enthusiasm and euphoria with which the opening of the wall was celebrated in both the FRG and the GDR, were soon replaced by much disillusionment and resentment in both the east and west and a process of more painful adjustment than the popular rush for unification had anticipated. While many former East Germans soon became disappointed with Western standards of living and quality of life, many former West Germans resented the seemingly ever-increasing cost of reunification. The initial days of idealism rapidly faded because of social and economic divisions between east and west. The biggest adjustments had to be made in the *Länder* of the former GDR whose political, social and economic systems had to adapt to those of the FRG. In the months which followed there were a host of problems to be addressed. These included disagreements over privatisation, uncompetitive industries, rising unemployment and fierce debates over '**destasification**'. The difficulties of adjustment lend, with hindsight, weight to the more moderate counsels of Modrow, who argued early in 1990 for a longer process towards reunification.

Destasification
The opening up of *Stasi* records to individuals and to the consideration of legal action against former *Stasi* employees.

Key term

Conclusion

So why was Germany reunited, and why at such a headlong rush, in 1990? The immediate and obvious answer is the force of the popular will: '*Wir Sind ein Volk*'. A revolution brought about by the power of a collective will, peacefully voiced. The momentum of the months from September 1989 appeared unstoppable. And yet a number of factors contributed both to the generation of that initial momentum and to the smoothing of its path to reunification. The stance and the policies of Gorbachev prior to September 1989 were key to the initial unlocking of the forces of liberalism and then protest. The decisions made at key points by individuals, chiefly Honecker, Kohl and Gorbachev, played a part. Above all we must remember the backdrop against which events unfolded. The growth of the Cold War in Europe was at the heart of the initial division of Germany. The end of the Cold War created the conditions which made reunification possible.

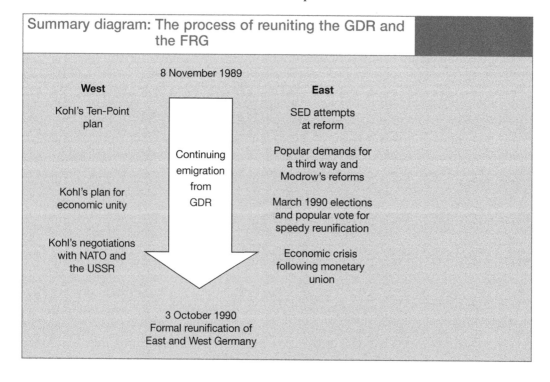

Summary diagram: The process of reuniting the GDR and the FRG

8 November 1989

West

Kohl's Ten-Point plan

Kohl's plan for economic unity

Kohl's negotiations with NATO and the USSR

Continuing emigration from GDR

East

SED attempts at reform

Popular demands for a third way and Modrow's reforms

March 1990 elections and popular vote for speedy reunification

Economic crisis following monetary union

3 October 1990
Formal reunification of East and West Germany

Key question
Why is Kohl sometimes referred to as the 'reunification Chancellor'?

6 | The Key Debate

How significant was Chancellor Kohl's contribution to the reuniting of Germany?

Historians are far from being in agreement over this. The historians Thomaneck and Niven think 'Kohl's reading of the situation and timing were astute and remarkable. Nevertheless, the epithet "Unification Chancellor", with which it has become customary to describe Kohl, is an overstatement'.

Kohl likened himself to **Bismarck** and took a lot of personal credit. Brandt, on the other hand, saw unification as the logical outcome of *Ostpolitik* which he had begun two decades earlier. Some US historians saw it as the achievement of the final aim of early Cold War policy (a united Germany as part of NATO). Historians such as Jarausch view these rapid events as due to the will of ordinary people, in contrast to Glees who sees the reuniting of Germany as a direct result of the actions of Kohl and Gorbachev.

Helmut Kohl was Chancellor of the FRG from 1982 to 1990 and of the reunited Germany from 1990 to 1998. This made him the first Chancellor since Adenauer to win four successive elections; by 1997, he was the longest serving Chancellor since Bismarck. He has been described as the 'reunification Chancellor,' and has become one of the most popular German politicians and a respected European statesman, a 'modern German Bismarck'. However, there are differing views as to his individual significance in the unification process. Some have seen Kohl as a pure opportunist. They argue that, without the particular developments in Eastern Europe and the USSR, the reuniting of Germany would not have been possible.

By the late 1980s Kohl's government was losing popularity. Throughout the summer of 1989 it was being widely predicted that in the forthcoming 1990 West German federal election, Kohl's CDU/CSU government would lose to the SPD. The chances of his being re-elected looked very unlikely, and there was also the distinct possibility that he would lose his leadership of the West German CDU. But the rapid chain of events which took place during 1989 and 1990 altered the CDU's fortunes radically and therefore, those of Kohl himself. It is in the light of these circumstances that some see him as an opportunist, seizing the moment to repair his political fortunes, rather than as a visionary statesman.

Key figure

Otto von Bismarck 1815–98
Chancellor of the German Empire from 1871 to 1890, Bismarck was the architect of German unification.

Kohl's initial caution regarding the reuniting of Germany

Key question
What did Kohl initially see as the risks in reuniting Germany?

Initially, during the summer and early autumn of 1989, Kohl had held crisis meetings to discuss events in Eastern Europe. At this point, it appeared that he wanted stability and that reunification was not his primary aim. He was being cautious, not wanting to inflame the situation in the GDR. Nor did he want thousands of East Germans emigrating to the FRG. Furthermore, he did not want to destabilise Eastern Europe and antagonise the USSR, thereby risking the stalling of the reform process occurring in much of Eastern Europe. He was also mindful that the *Stasi* still existed in the GDR, with powers to arrest and imprison East German citizens. However, by November, there were increasing chants from protesters of 'we are one people', and President Bush had by now made it clear that the USA would not resist Germany's reuniting. Events inside the GDR and internationally both encouraged reunification.

Differing views of Kohl's role in the reuniting of Germany

Kohl the 'architect of unification?' Was Kohl responsible for the reuniting of Germany?

Kohl is seen by some historians, such as Gerhard Wettig, as the architect of German reunification and a visionary statesman, who continued the process of Brandt's *Ostpolitik*. His initial sense of caution in the early part of the autumn of 1989 seems to have been due to his very real concerns about the safety of individuals in the GDR, as well as anxiety over the ability of the West German economy and its people to assimilate the influx of citizens from the GDR. However, his personal intervention in rapidly drawing up the Ten-Point Plan for the reunification of Germany in November 1989, and his swift and crucial meeting with Gorbachev, can be seen as his taking control and steering towards reunification. Kohl's intervention, although dashing Modrow's plans for a future German confederation, indicates his astute reading of the popular mood within the GDR and the sheer numbers of East Germans who were voting with their feet. He was then able to use the East German election results in March 1990 to secure a strong negotiating position at an international level with both the USSR and the Western Allies – a necessary prerequisite before the FRG and GDR could enter into any official agreements themselves.

Kohl the opportunist? Was Kohl seizing on events for his own advantage?

The title of 'unification Chancellor' can be seen as 'an overstatement'. Kohl may have realised that the reuniting of Germany was going to occur at some point, and, aware of his increasing unpopularity in the FRG, exploited developments elsewhere to increase his own status and prospects for re-election. As an opportunist, he then used the sheer economic power of the FRG to make rash economic promises to East Germans, and to buy off a cash-stricken USSR. His serious underestimation of the costs of reuniting Germany (deliberate or otherwise) only served to bring rapid disillusionment in the former East and West Germanys.

Fortunate circumstances: the decline of the GDR

On the other hand the GDR's long-term decline can be emphasised and Kohl seen as the beneficiary of fortunate circumstances, rather than as the architect of them either as visionary or as opportunist. This interpretation sees him as in the right place at the right time. Hans-Hermann Hertle argues that the GDR government was simply unable to continue. As a result of its spiralling economic problems, it was already vulnerable when Gorbachev came to power. The SED's reluctance to intervene in the demonstrations in Leipzig on 8–9 October, Honecker's removal from power, and the opening of the Berlin Wall: all these show that the East German government was increasingly lacking in confidence and had become fatally weakened.

US historian Henry Ashby-Turner also places emphasis on the long-term decline of the GDR, caused by the policy of 'transformation through *rapprochement*' – initiated by Brandt's *Ostpolitik* and continued by Schmidt and Kohl. Ashby-Turner claims that this undermined the SED's ability to sustain its acceptance among East Germans. This 'loss of plausibility', together with generous aid from the West and a widening material gap, contributed to the 'profound estrangement of East Germans from their government that came to expression in the autumn of 1989'.

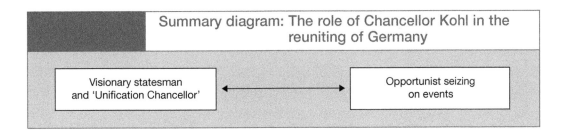

Summary diagram: The role of Chancellor Kohl in the reuniting of Germany

Visionary statesman and 'Unification Chancellor' ⟷ Opportunist seizing on events

Some key books in the debate
A. Glees, *Reinventing Germany* (Berg, 1996)
K. Jarausch, *The Rush to German Unity* (Oxford, 1994)
J. Thomaneck and B. Niven, *Dividing and Uniting Germany* (Routledge, 2001)

Postscript: A Reunited Germany Dealing with its Past and its Future

The sudden appearance of a new reunited Germany in 1990 threw up a range of debates and controversies. The reuniting of Germany required individuals to adapt to new social, political and economic structures. It brought with it the need for many East Germans to make considerable adjustments at the level of the mundane and the profound. For example, former East German citizens were amazed at how many varieties of toilet rolls they saw when they first visited the West, former East German builders were amazed that materials could be delivered the very same day, and others were horrified to find that trusted friends and family members had informed on them and had been responsible for their imprisonment.

This study focuses on one particular nation, but it is also important to consider the reuniting of Germany in a wider global context. Some analysts would see it as the end of the legacies of the Second World War and very much part of a historical process that occurred throughout the whole of Eastern Europe and the USSR. It may be seen as the liberation of many people from living under the controls and repression of socialism and an end to living under the tensions of a Cold War between two heavily armed superpowers. Nevertheless, since the end of the Cold War many have found their lives to be more precarious and less certain. A significantly enlarged post-Cold War NATO has also brought new international tensions and uncertainty.

In Germany itself today, very little remains of the Berlin Wall. In central Berlin the wall's remnants are a line of cobbled stones showing its former course, with a few small sections preserved to serve as memorials and monuments. At various points, simple crosses commemorate the lives lost during the attempted crossings between 1961 and 1989. When the wall was taken down, much of the wall was used for building roads. Some parts of it are now in various museums around the world, including the Imperial War Museum in London. In the autumn of 2008 a Berlin auction house sold a remaining section of the Berlin Wall to a private company for more than £6000. While some have welcomed its destruction as an opportunity to create a new Germany, others have argued that it marks the brushing away of the past.

The legacy of the *Stasi*

When the Berlin Wall opened in 1989 *Stasi* officers hastily destroyed as many of the classified documents as they could. They worked so frantically that the shredding machines broke down. The files that survived were later made accessible to former citizens of the GDR. No secret police force in history has ever spied on its own people on the scale of the *Stasi*; in East Germany there was one informer to every seven citizens. One former East German citizen found that more than 80 people had been spying on her at some point in her life. Side by side, the files would have stretched more than 180 km.

More than 600 million scraps of paper were retrieved filling more than 16,000 sacks. A team of 36 six people was set up in 1995 to try and piece together as much of the paper as possible. They managed 300 sacks in the first six years and averaged 10 documents a day simply using tape and tweezers. It was estimated that it would take up to 400 years to complete the task, but by 2008, with computers being used to match the fragments, it was recalculated that the task would be completed by 2013. There have been requests for the technology developed to be used in other former Eastern bloc states such as Latvia and Poland.

'Wessis' and 'Ossis'

Since the reuniting of Germany, there has been a change from the initial euphoria with which it was first greeted in both Germanys and there was later a rise of ***Ostalgie*** in the east. The '***Wessis***' often stereotyped the '***Ossis***' as ungrateful, lazy and lacking initiative, while the '***Ossis***' saw '***Wessis***' as materialistic and self-absorbed. Some East Germans reminisce about the security of employment, cheap housing and lower crime rates that life in GDR had offered them. Many Germans still talk of the continued wall that remains fixed 'in your head'.

A belief developed among some West Germans that any East Germans with initiative or self-motivation had already had already left the GDR prior to the building of the wall. Those living in the two Germanys had actually developed two very different sets of values. In the West personal freedom meant the freedom of speech, of assembly and of travel. For those in the East, freedom meant security from the threats of unemployment, crime and homelessness.

Ostalgie

The growth in so-called *Ostalgie* can be seen as an attempt by former East Germans to deal with the insecurities they faced in a reunited Germany. This created a series of television chat shows, and the opening of a private museum in central Berlin devoted solely to the recreation of daily life in the former GDR. There is now even a hotel *Ostotel* with clocks displaying the world time in Berlin, Beijing, Havana and Moscow. A Berlin pub opened in 2008 in Normannenstrasse, the former headquarters of the Ministry for State Security. The pub is decorated with *Stasi*

Key terms

Ostalgie
Nostalgia for life in the former GDR. *Ost* is the German word for east.

Wessis
A colloquial term often used disparagingly to refer to those Germans from the former FRG.

Ossis
A colloquial term often used disparagingly to refer to those Germans from the former GDR.

memorabilia including an urn which, the owners claim, contains Honecker's ashes.

Others fear that this nostalgic view of the past makes some forget the darker side of life in the GDR. Former GDR political prisoners work as tour guides in what had been the notorious Hohenschönhausen *Stasi* prison. Over four decades, tens of thousands of political prisoners had been locked away there and subjected to psychological torture. However, an organisation was established in the early 1990s to protest against the criminal charges being made against former *Stasi* members. They argued that the charges were 'victor's justice' and called for them to be dropped. Today the group calls for the closure of the Hohenschönhausen museum.

Berlin as the capital of a new Germany

In June 1991, the German *Bundestag*, after a heated debate, voted narrowly for Berlin to become the capital of Germany once more, and for both the German federal government and parliament to return there. The former *Reichstag* became the seat of the German *Bundestag*. Since the *Reichstag* fire in February 1933, the building had been used only rarely, and had been heavily damaged by bombing during the Second World War. It was restored in 1956 but had been used only for occasional meetings. It temporarily housed an exhibition of German history in the early 1980s. It was restored as the home of the German *Bundestag* in 1999. The refurbishment included a glass dome to symbolise open and transparent government. Another iconic building is the famous Kaiser Wilhelm Memorial Church in Berlin, built in 1895, most of which had been destroyed during an air raid in November 1943. It has stood as a ruin to serve as a reminder of the devastation of much of Berlin during the Second World War. Now the problems of erosion and lack of funds for repair may mean that it has to be taken down.

A new Germany as a global power

On the international stage Germany seems to have established a new sense of confidence and national identity. German troops have been deployed with United Nations' forces in Afghanistan and Kosovo. The deployment of German troops abroad would have been unthinkable before the very late twentieth century. Germany has also been confident enough to distance itself from the USA and it declined to send troops under US-led foreign policy to the first and second Gulf Wars. In November 2007, the former West German Chancellor, Helmut Schmidt, wrote in the German newspaper *Die Zeit* that the USA was a greater threat to world peace than Russia. He argued that Russia had not invaded its neighbours since the end of the Cold War and that he was surprised that Russia allowed Ukraine and other former components of the USSR to secede peacefully. He noted that the US invasion of Iraq under George W. Bush was 'a war of choice, not a war of necessity'.

Recent German films' attempt to deal with the past

In recent years there have been some internationally recognised films from Germany:

- *Sonnenallee* was made in 1999 and is a comedy about East Berlin teenagers' running up against the GDR authorities for welcoming visits from a West Berlin relative.
- *Goodbye Lenin* was another major international success in 2002. Set in East Berlin, the film is about a mother, a devout SED supporter, falling into a coma after seeing her son in the autumn 1989 demonstrations. When she awakes, her son becomes involved in elaborate deception to avoid shocking her with the news of reunification. He also traces his father who had long before left home for West Berlin.
- The award-winning 2006 film *The Lives of Others* deals with the *Stasi* and its surveillance of citizens in East Berlin and includes scenes depicting Hohenschönhausen prison and the training of *Stasi* officers.

Individuals and the recent past: two Germans' personal experiences

There are two accounts below. In the first, Jutta reminds us that the decisions made by nation states have profound effects on individual experiences. In the second, Maria's story mirrors the larger experiences of Germany itself. Post-war poverty and dislocation were followed by a more stable and prosperous existence born of sheer hard work.

Jutta Scholz

Jutta Scholz was born in Berlin in 1934 and had moved to England in 1953 to marry a man she had met when he was serving with the British armed forces in Berlin. Until 2008 she had felt her own personal story was of no importance and interest and that people might even accuse her of making it up.

When the Second World War ended, she witnessed a Soviet soldier holding a pistol to her father's head and asking for money and jewellery. Somehow, his life was spared, and her mother was saved from being raped. Jutta scavenged for food, saw the piles of corpses in the streets and bodies hung from lamp-posts. She remembers the dirty water, the cholera, the lice, and having to walk miles into the countryside to collect apples. She recalls the banknotes being worthless, the generosity of US soldiers, and catching sweets dropped from US aircraft during the Berlin Blockade.

Jutta's earlier childhood memories include being evacuated to live with her grandmother in rural eastern Germany, and then returning to her mother and father (who had been invalided out of the forces) in Berlin in November 1944. She speaks of how she proudly she wore her German Maidens' uniform and enjoyed that movement's social activities, although her mother did not approve. Jutta explained that she had a sense of things 'not being talked about'. In the final stages of the war, she experienced the nightly air raids from a child's viewpoint; to her the time spent in cellar seemed 'normal'.

After the Second World War, she moved to England and, until the 1970s, faced hostility from many English civilians. She cried profusely when the wall came down. Even though she was only a young girl during the Third Reich she still feels shame and guilt at being German even after choosing to move to England. She still suffers from frequent nightmare images of Berlin during and immediately after the Second World War.

Maria Klemm

Maria Klemm lived with her mother and five siblings in the town of Dörnsdorf which was taken over by Czechoslovakia at the end of the war and is now called Dolina. Her father had served in the *Wehrmacht* but nobody knows where and how he died.

Maria remembers one particular night sometime in April 1946. Armed Czechs stood in the door of their house and ordered her family to leave immediately. They were put on carts pulled by cows and horses, and then on to cargo train wagons which had straw-covered floors. After what felt like a very long time, they arrived in Friedrichsdorf, a town in Hesse in the American zone of occupied Germany. With many others, they were taken to a school hall. The refugees were then divided up to stay with local families. Nobody wanted a family with six children, so they were

At the end of the war large sections of Berlin were in ruins. The children are playing here in front of the ruins of the former *Reich* Chancellery in 1946. The writing on the building reads, 'Never Again – Therefore SED'. What do you think was meant by this slogan?

given two rooms in a local hat factory. Meanwhile her uncle, with his wife and two children, had ended up in the Eastern zone. Maria's mother convinced the mayor that they could all stay in those two rooms in the hat factory. Several months later the uncle and his family were allowed to come from the eastern zone and stay in Friedrichsdorf.

Maria's mother found a job as a cleaner in a factory. Maria and her siblings went to school in the mornings. Each day after school, their mother passed on to them the lunch the factory provided for her. When the serving lady learnt about that sacrifice, she always gave Maria's mother an extra spoonful. Maria remembers that there was a great deal of work to be done. Children contributed as well. After school they always worked; mainly planting and harvesting in the fields. In the 1950s the family were given compensation of about DM4000 or DM5000 by the state for having lost their house back in Dörnsdorf. The town of Friedrichsdorf made cheap building land available to refugees and the family was able to build a home and a new life. They worked very hard and Maria maintains that is how they made their new life in the FRG successful.

A memorial of wooden black crosses to more than 1000 individuals who had been killed trying to cross the Berlin Wall was erected near Checkpoint Charlie in central Berlin in 2004 but was pulled down by court order in 2005. At the very front of the photograph there is an inscription to Peter Fechter. Why do you think this memorial was taken down?

Further Reading

Chapter 1

M. Fulbrook, *The Two Germanies, 1945–1990; Problems of Interpretation* (Macmillan, 1992)

V. Klemperer, *I Shall Bear Witness 1933–41, To The Bitter End 1941–45, The Lesser Evil 1945–59* (Phoenix, 1999)

W. Loth, *Stalin's Unwanted Child*, (Palgrave, 1998)

A. McDougall, 'A duty to forget? The Hitler youth generation', *German History* Vol. 26, No. 1, 2008

Chapter 2

W. Gray, *Germany's Cold War: The Global Campaign to Isolate East Germany* (North Carolina Press, 2003)

A. Hildebrandt, *The Wall: Facts and Figures* (Haus am Checkpoint Charlie, 2005)

K. Jarausch, *After Hitler: Recivilizing Germans 1945–95* (Oxford, 2006)

O. Kirchheimer, 'Germany: the vanishing opposition' in R.A. Dahl (editor) *Political Oppositions in Western Democracies* (Yale, 1966)

G. Kwiatkowski, 'Peasants revolt? Re-evaluating the 17 June uprising', *German History* Vol. 24, No. 2, 2006

J. Madarasz, *Conflict and Compromise in East Germany* (Palgrave Macmillan, 2003)

P. Major, *The Workers' and Peasants' State* (Manchester, 2002)

S. Stern, *Marshall Plan 1947–1997* (Inter Nationes, 1997)

Chapter 3

M. Fulbrook, *History of Germany 1918–2000* (Blackwell, 2002)

A. Glees, *Reinventing Germany* (Berg, 1996)

K. Larres and P. Panayi, *The Federal Republic of Germany since 1949* (Longman, 1996)

A. Nichols, *The Bonn Republic* (Longman, 1997)

Chapter 4

D. Childs, *The Fall of the GDR* (Longman, 2001)

M. Fulbrook, *The People's State: East German Society from Hitler to Honecker* (Yale, 2005)

M. Fulbrook, *Anatomy of a Dictatorship* (Oxford, 1995)

M. Fulbrook, *A History of Germany 1918–2008* (Blackwell, 2009)

A. Port, *Conflict and Stability in the GDR* (Cambridge, 2007)

H. Schwarze, *The GDR Today* (Köln, 1970)

M. Simmons, *The Unloved Country* (Abacus, 1989)

Chapter 5

H. Ashby-Turner, *Germany from Partition to Reunification* (Yale, 1982)

S. Crawshaw, *Easier Fatherland* (Continuum, 2004)

M. Dennis, *The Rise and Fall of the German Democratic Republic, 1945–1990* (Longman, 2000)

M. Fulbrook, *Anatomy of a Dictatorship: Inside the GDR 1949–89* (Oxford, 1995)

M. Fulbrook, *History of Germany 1918–2000* (Blackwell, 2002)

A. Glees, *Reinventing Germany* (Berg, 1996)

K. Jarausch, *The Rush to German Unity* (Oxford, 1994)

L Kettenacker, *Germany Since 1945* (Opus, 1997)

J. McAdams, *Germany Divided* (Princeton, 1993)

J. Thomaneck and B. Niven, *Dividing and Uniting Germany* (Routledge, 2001)

G. Wettig, *The Soviet Union and German Unification* (Berichte des Bundesinstituts, 1990)

Glossary

Alexanderplatz A major square in Berlin which became the centre of East Berlin. It witnessed the largest public demonstration in the GDR on 4 November 1989.

Allied High Commission Set up under the Basic Treaty, it retained ultimate authority over the constitution and the legislation of the FRG.

Anti-Bolshevik The Bolsheviks, led by Lenin, had taken power in Russia in 1917. Anti-Bolshevism was a fundamental part of Nazi ideology.

Anti-fascist protective wall The official name given by the GDR government to the inner-German border and later to the Berlin Wall.

Baby boom The sudden increase in the post-war birth rate. By the early 1970s those born in immediate post-war years were of working age.

Basic Law The constitution of the newly formed FRG.

Battle for Berlin The name commonly given to the final few months of the Second World War in Europe which led to Soviet forces finally occupying the city itself.

Battle of Stalingrad A major Soviet victory, 1942–3, over Germany during the Second World War, which marked a downturn in Germany's military fortunes.

Beer Hall *Putsch* Hitler's failed attempt in Munich in November 1923 to overthrow the Bavarian government.

Brezhnev Doctrine The USSR claimed the right to intervene in Eastern bloc states to maintain the unity of the Warsaw Pact.

Bundesbank The FRG's central bank.

Bundeswehr The FRG's armed forces were set up in 1955 with initially only a defensive role.

Checkpoint Charlie A crossing point between East and West Berlin. It was the only border crossing that could be used by both visitors and Allied forces. In the East it was called the Zimmermann Strasse border crossing.

Co-determination The principle that workers would be represented at management levels in industry to help develop and maintain sound industrial relations by co-operation and negotiation.

Cold War The period of hostility, but not outright war, between the USA and USSR and their Allies from the end of the Second World War until the early 1990s.

Collectivisation Private farms being taken over by state co-operatives.

COMECON The economic organisation of the Eastern bloc and the USSR, set up in 1949.

COMINFORM The Communist Information Bureau. Set up in 1947 by the USSR to organise communist infiltration and intelligence gathering in non-communist states.

Construction soldiers Men who refused conscription to the GDR's armed forces and instead did hard physical labour on projects such as building roads and housing.

Cuban Missile Crisis A serious confrontation in 1962 between the USA and the USSR after Soviet nuclear bases were found to have been installed in Cuba.

Decartelisation The reduction in the power and influence of big business interests that had supported the Nazi government.

Denazification The process of ridding Germany of the conditions and individuals that were responsible for Nazism.

Destasification The opening up of *Stasi* records to individuals and to the consideration of legal action against former *Stasi* employees.

Détente The reduction in tension between the USA and the USSR from the late 1960s to the early 1980s.

Eastern bloc The collective name given to the socialist states in Eastern Europe allied to the USSR.

Eastern Front The scene of military conflict between Germany and the USSR, including much of Eastern Europe, during the Second World War.

EEC European Economic Community – the forerunner of today's European Union.

Federal Republic of Germany Otherwise referred to as West Germany or *Bundesrepublik Deutschland* with its capital in Bonn. It officially existed from May 1949 until October 1990.

German Democratic Republic Otherwise referred to as East Germany or *Deutsche Demokratische Republik*. Its capital was referred to as East Berlin by the West, but as 'Berlin – Capital of the GDR' by the East. It officially existed from October 1949 until October 1990.

Greek Civil War Following occupation by Nazi Germany there was a civil war, 1946–9, between the government and communist forces.

Guest workers The name given to workers who came to the FRG from Turkey and other parts of southern Europe.

Hard currency A currency that the market considers to be strong because its value does not fall, in this case the *Deutschemark*.

Helsinki Accords A series of agreements signed by 35 European states as well as the USSR and the USA in 1975, aimed at improving international relations.

IM *Inoffizielle Mitarbeiter*: individuals often recruited by the *Stasi* on a temporary basis to gather information and report their findings.

Inflation A process in which money declines in value and prices rise as a consequence.

Iron Curtain A term popularised in 1946 by Winston Churchill, Britain's wartime Prime Minister, to describe the increasing division of Europe between east and west.

July Bomb Plot The attempted assassination of Hitler by German army officers in 1944.

Kristallnacht The destruction during the Third Reich of many Jewish businesses, synagogues and homes throughout Germany on 9 November 1938.

NATO The North Atlantic Treaty Organisation. A military alliance set up in 1949. It was made up of countries in Western Europe as well as the USA and Canada.

Neues Deutschland The official East German SED newspaper which promoted party policy.

Niche society People showing loyalty towards the state and socialism in public, while developing personal fulfilment and interests within close-knit family and friendship groups.

NPD National German Party: a right-wing political party formed in 1964, which gained some seats in state elections in the later 1960s.

Nuremberg Laws A series of anti-Jewish laws passed in Nazi Germany in 1935; included the prohibition of sexual relations and marriage between Jews and Aryans.

Oder–Neisse Rivers on the eastern side of Germany.

OPEC Organisation of Petroleum Exporting Counties: a largely Middle Eastern oil cartel.

Ossis A colloquial term often used disparagingly to refer to those Germans from the former GDR.

Ostalgie Nostalgia for life in the former GDR. *Ost* is the German word for east.

Ostpolitik 'Eastern policy': an attempt to normalise relations between West Germany and the Eastern bloc.

Plattenbauen Buildings made from concrete slabs.

Policy of strength A policy especially associated with Adenauer. It sought to increase the FRG's military and economic strength in order to put them in a stronger position to counter socialism.

Politburo The most senior executive and policy-making committee in the SED ruling government in East Germany.

Pravda The official government newspaper in the USSR.

Rapprochement Developing contact and relations by diplomacy and agreement.

Reichstag The German Parliament building until 1933 and then again following the reunification of Germany.

Reparations Payments by Germany as compensation for the damage caused during the Second World War.

Revisionist Historians whose views challenge former commonly accepted opinions.

Round Table A group set up in December 1989 with members from both the East German *Volkskammer* and opposition groups to discuss government policies.

Self-determination The right of nations to govern themselves, free from control by another power.

SMAD The Soviet Military Administration which controlled the USSR's occupation of the Eastern zone.

Social market The combination of free, capitalist markets and the state's protection of workers' rights and welfare.

Socialist state In this instance, the following of Marxist–Leninist ideology by many countries in post-war Eastern Europe, which are also often referred to as communist.

Solidarity An anti-socialist trade union, which began in Poland in the early 1980s and influenced the growth of reform movements throughout Eastern Europe.

Spiegel affair A scandal following the revelation that journalists working for *Spiegel* magazine were arrested after criticising the FRG's armed forces.

Stalinallee A major street in East Berlin, later named Karl-Marx Allee as part of de-Stalinisation in 1961. Its spacious apartments remained desirable throughout the history of the GDR.

Stalinist Ruthless single-party control, as in the USSR.

Star Wars Project The development of space-based systems to protect the USA from nuclear missile attacks.

Stasi GDR's Ministry for State Security, set up in 1950, which developed extensive surveillance both within the GDR and internationally.

Tempelhof Airport A commercial airport until October 2008. On its final day of operation elderly Berliners held placards stating 'Thank you America'.

Totalitarian A form of government in which the state has total control over its society and people.

Treaty of Brest-Litovsk The punitive peace treaty imposed by Germany on Russia in 1918.

Treaty of Versailles The 1919 settlement that forced Germany to give up territory, pay reparations, reduce its armed forces, and accept responsibility for the First World War.

Two plus Four   The two Germanys and the four powers from the Second World War.

Ulbricht Group   German communists who had been in exile in the USSR when Hitler was in power. After Germany's surrender, they began developing the Eastern zone along socialist lines under directives from Stalin.

Warsaw Ghetto   The largest Jewish ghetto in Nazi-occupied Europe. Between 1940 and 1943 a large proportion of its half a million inhabitants died from disease or starvation or were transported to Nazi extermination camps.

Warsaw Pact   Set up in 1955 as a military alliance of Eastern European socialist states by the USSR in response to FRG's membership of NATO.

Wehrmacht   The German armed forces from 1935 to 1945.

Wessis   A colloquial term often used disparagingly to refer to those Germans from the former FRG.

Yalta   The wartime conference of February 1945 which decided that the countries in Eastern Europe that had been invaded by Germany should be re-established after the war.

Yom Kippur War   Also known as the Fourth Arab–Israeli War, when Egypt and Syria led a largely unsuccessful attack against Israel in October 1973.

Zionism   The movement for establishing an independent state of Israel.

Index